Marching Toward Freedom

The Library of American History
General Editor: John Anthony Scott

Marching Toward Freedom

BLACKS IN THE CIVIL WAR
1861–1865

James M. McPherson

Illustrated with contemporary prints
and photographs

Facts On File
New York • Oxford

Marching Toward Freedom

Facts On File, Inc.
460 Park Avenue South
New York NY 10016
USA

Facts On File Limited
Collins Street
Oxford OX4 1XJ
United Kingdom

Library of Congress Cataloging-in-Publication Data
McPherson, James M.
    Marching toward freedom : blacks in the Civil War, 1861–1865 / James M. McPherson.
        p.   cm.
        Includes bibliographical references (p.   ) and index.   Summary: Using a wide variety of primary sources, examines the   Afro-Americans' role in the contribution to the Union and   Confederacy
during the Civil War the resulting change in their   position as citizens.
        ISBN 0-8160-2337-9 : $16.95.
        1. United States—History—Civil War, 1861–1865—Afro-Americans—Juvenile literature. [1. United States—History—Civil War, 1861–1865—Afro-Americans. 2. Afro-Americans—History.] I. Title.
        E540.N3M24   1991
        973.7'150396073—dc20   90-13918

A British CIP catalogue record for this book is available from the British Library.

Facts On File books are available at special discounts when purchased in bulk quantities for businesses, associations, institutions or sales promotions. Please call our Special Sales Department in New York at 212/683-2244 (dial 800/322-8755 except in NY, AK or HI) or in Oxford at 865/728399.

Text design by Donna Sinisgalli
Jacket design by Soloway/Mitchell Associates
Composition by Facts On File, Inc.
Manufactured by The Maple-Vail Book Manufacturing Group
Printed in the United States of America

10 9 8 7 6 5 4 3 2 1

This book is printed on acid-free paper.

For David and John

CONTENTS

INTRODUCTION

When the original edition of this book was published in 1967, the United States was experiencing race riots at home and an unpopular war in Vietnam—in which African-American soldiers bore a large share of the fighting. The 1960s were a decade of extraordinary racial tension and violence—but also of extraordinary progress in the legal status of black people. The civil rights movement won great victories in the desegregation of public facilities and the political mobilization of southern blacks, culminating in the Civil Rights Act of 1964 and the Voting Rights Act of 1965. These achievements built up expectations of similar progress in the economic and social status of blacks. When the reality fell short of expectations, the resulting frustration exploded into riots in many cities during the long, hot summer of 1967.

If the 1960s were marked by both violence and progress in race relations, the Civil War exactly a century earlier was characterized by a level of intensity manyfold greater in both violence and progress. At least 620,000 soldiers and sailors lost their lives in the Civil War, which preserved the existence of an undivided United States and abolished slavery, thereby liberating four million African-Americans and their descendants from bondage. Northern victory in the war laid the foundation of equal rights for the freed slaves embodied in the Fourteenth and Fifteenth

Amendments to the Constitution, passed during the years just after the war and finally enforced a century later.

The Civil War marks the greatest single turning point in the history of African-Americans. But for a long time, many people were not aware of how active and vital a role blacks themselves played in making it so important. In 1928, one historian expressed a common misconception:

American negroes are the only people in the history of the world, so far as I know, that ever became free without any effort of their own . . . [The Civil War] was not their business. They had not started the war nor ended it. They twanged banjos around the railroad stations, sang melodious spirituals, and believed that some Yankee would soon come along and give each of them forty acres of land and a mule.

This statement could not have been more wrong. The reader of the following pages will soon learn the crucial part hundreds of thousands of African-Americans played in winning their freedom—and in helping the North win the war and preserve the Union. Slave "contrabands" took the first step toward freedom by coming into Union lines and forcing the emancipation question on the Union government. Northern black leaders and abolitionists kept the freedom question before the public. Some 190,000 African-Americans fought in the Union army and navy; 37,000 of them gave their lives for the Union and freedom. Many thousands of others worked as teamsters, laborers and the like for the Union army. Without the labor power and fighting power of these black men, as Abraham Lincoln himself said in 1864, "We can not longer maintain the contest. . . . We would be compelled to abandon the war."

Revised and updated since its first publication 24 years ago, this book makes clear the vital part that African-Americans took in the Civil War. It is important for all Americans to know about these events, not only for an understanding of that greatest of all crises in American history but also for an understanding of race relations today, which are no less central to our society in 1991 than

they were when the book was first published in 1967 or
when the events chronicled in these pages took place.

James M. McPherson
Princeton, New Jersey

PREFACE

Millions of American young people passing through our schools and colleges learn their United States history almost exclusively from standard textbooks. Growing dissatisfaction with these texts was eloquently voiced when Frances Fitzgerald published *America Revised: History Schoolbooks in the Twentieth Century* in 1979. High school history texts, Fitzgerald charged, are supremely dull and uninteresting. They fail to hold the atttention of the young people or to fire their imagination. United States history ought to arouse wonder, compassion and delight, but these books turn it into a crashing bore. One of the reasons for this, she said, is that the texts do not often draw upon the marvelous original sources that this nation inherits, which constitute the lifeblood of history, and which are indispensable to its study, no matter what the age of the student.

Efforts to find alternatives to the traditional texts began some years before Fitzgerald's book appeared. One of these was an initiative that Alfred A. Knopf launched in 1966. The result was the publication, during the years 1967–77, of an historical series designed for the use of high school students and of undergraduates and entitled The Living History Library. In all, fifteen volumes were published in this series. Each book was written by a distinguished historian or teacher. Each told the story of a different period or topic in American history—the colonial period, the American Revolution, the black experience in the Civil

War, the cowboy in the West, the Great Depression, and so on. Each was based upon original sources woven throughout into the framework of the narrative. Ordinary people who witnessed historical events and participated in historical struggles provided their own testimony and told their own story both in word and song. The series presented the American experience through the medium of a new literary art form. People long dead and struggles long past came to life again in the present.

The historical and literary value of these books has not diminished with the passage of time. On the contrary, the need for books such as these is greater today than it has ever been before. Innumerable important topics in our history await treatment of this type. Facts On File is happy to publish new and updated editions of the Living History Library books as part of its own Library of American History.

Marching Toward Freedom is the story of how black soldiers, from both the North and the South, fought to win their own freedom from slavery and to smash the grip of the slaveholders upon the American Union. At the outbreak of the war the Union army did not accept black volunteers; African-Americans had to find other ways to serve their country. Some worked as spies, cooks, teachers and nurses, while others, fleeing the plantations, joined the Union armies to work as laborers. All this changed in 1863 when the first all-black regiments were recruited, trained and sent into battle. In July of that year the 54th Massachusetts Regiment (Colored) led the assault upon Fort Wagner in South Carolina; this was for the black soldiers of the Civil War what Bunker Hill had been for the revolutionaries of 1775. The superlative military record of the black troops spelled the dawning of a new day for all African-Americans in their struggle for human rights and equality in America.

Marching Toward Freedom

1

LESS THAN A CITIZEN
African-Americans Before the Civil War

In a historic decision, the United States Supreme Court ruled in 1857 that Dred Scott, being a black man, was therefore not a citizen of the United States. The ruling did not surprise most Americans, for in very few parts of the United States did black people have any rights that whites were bound to respect.

In the South, 4,000,000 slaves were, in the eyes of the law, articles of property rather than human beings. They could be bought and sold at the will of a master. Slaves had no right of legal marriage, and by law a slave child belonged not to his parents, but to his white master. Families could be, and often were, separated. The laws gave white men large powers of punishment over slaves, ¿nd many blacks bore the scars of whippings on their backs.

Slavery was a terrible thing. The worst part of it was not the master's physical power over his slave, but the narrow mental and spiritual world in which most bondsmen lived. An educated slave was a dangerous slave, so it was in the master's interest to keep his blacks as ignorant as possible. All the Southern states had laws against teaching slaves to read and write. Consequently nearly all of them were illiterate, and those few who could read had learned secretly. Slaves could not own property; they could not testify against white persons in court; they could not leave their master's premises without written permission. Uneducated and powerless in a society dominated by slaveowners, they lived in ignorance and hopelessness, without plans for the future or any chance to control their own destinies.

For them, each day was like the last, and the days, weeks and years stretched on in an endless train of drudgery and dullness. Most slaves had only the vaguest notion of what the world outside their own plantation was like. Since they had always been slaves and, so far as they knew, always would be, they had little idea that any other condition was possible for them.

The condition of the 250,000 *free* blacks in the South was little better. They could not vote and had few civil rights. They were segregated in almost every aspect of their lives, and were seldom allowed a chance to get ahead. There were no public schools for them, so, with the exception of a few thousand blacks in cities like New Orleans and Charleston who had managed to acquire wealth and education, the free blacks of the South were almost as illiterate as the slaves.

The 225,000 blacks of the North were somewhat better off. In most states they could attend public schools; they could organize societies to improve their condition; they had some hope of getting ahead in life. But their opportunities were narrow and their rights limited, for a Jim Crow—that is, segregated—system had put them at the bottom of the social scale.

Except in New England, most Northern public school systems were segregated. Trains, streetcars, restaurants and hotels in many parts of the North were also segregated, and there was discrimination everywhere in jobs and housing. Some states did not allow African-Americans to testify against whites in court, and they could vote in only a few states. Race prejudice in the North was strong, especially among Irish immigrants and lower-class whites competing with blacks in an effort to rise from the bottom of society. If black people were not citizens at all in the South, in the North they were definitely second-class citizens.

Yet there were white people in both North and South who disliked slavery and discrimination. In the South few dared speak out for fear of being branded traitors to the Southern way of life; but some secretly defied the system by teaching slaves to read or by helping them escape. There were masters who had guilt feelings about slavery and were kinder to their slaves than the law prescribed.

In the North, an outspoken group of people called abolitionists denounced slavery, urged the emancipation of the slaves and tried to secure equal rights for free blacks. Other Northerners did not go so far as the abolitionists but nevertheless considered slavery a bad institution and wished that something could be done about it, although they did not know what to do. From 1845 to 1860, there was a growing feeling in the North against slavery. It was due not so much to concern for the slaves themselves as to fear of the South's political power in the national government and to a belief that slavery should be kept out of the territories, so that when they came into the Union, they would do so as free states. Most people in the North hoped that slavery would eventually disappear from the United States, enabling America to fulfill the promise of freedom for all contained in the Declaration of Independence.

Then, in 1854, the Republican Party was born. It was an antislavery party in that it wanted to keep slavery out of new territories and states, but it did not propose to abolish slavery where it already existed. Nevertheless, the South feared that the Republican Party would eventually threaten the whole Southern way of life; and when Abraham Lincoln was elected president in 1860, Southern states began seceding from the Union. On April 12, 1861, Confederate cannons bombarded Fort Sumter, firing the first shots in a bloody and destructive four-year Civil War. The South had shown itself willing to fight to preserve its institutions—and slavery.

From then on—from the surrender of Fort Sumter to the surrender at Appomattox—the question of slavery's status in a restored Union occupied much of the attention of the

Northern people and their leaders. The "Negro Question" was to become one of the main issues of the war; and the Americans most affected by the war would be black people, slave and free. A writer in an antislavery newspaper declared in 1863 that the black was "the observed of all observers; the talked of by all talkers; the thought of by all thinkers; and the questioned by all questioners."

2

"THIS IS A WHITE MAN'S WAR"

Though the South was willing to fight to preserve slavery, the North at first was *not* willing to fight to destroy slavery. In 1861–1862, the overriding Northern war aim was, simply and clearly, the restoration of the Union. Although President Lincoln personally hated slavery, he needed the support of people in the North and in the border slave states (Kentucky, Missouri, Maryland and Delaware) who upheld a war to preserve the Union but would not support a war to abolish slavery. Therefore Lincoln said several times in the first year of the war that he had no intention of interfering with the "domestic institutions" of the South and that he only wanted to restore the Union as it had been before 1861—that is, a Union with slavery still existing in the South.

Nevertheless, in the first weeks after the fall of Fort Sumter, Northern blacks joined in the general outburst of patriotism and offered their services to the Union government. Black soldiers had fought in the American Revolution and the War of 1812, and their grandsons were ready to help defend the country once more. Northern blacks welcomed the coming of hostilities, hoping, in spite of Lincoln's statements, that the conflict would eventually bring about the downfall of slavery. After all, they reasoned, the Confederacy was fighting *for* slavery, and the North must soon realize it could not win the war without fighting *against* slavery. So, in Boston, New York, Philadelphia, Pittsburgh and other cities, black men began to organize militia companies.

But race prejudice was still so strong in the North in 1861 that white leaders—from the secretary of war down to local militia officers—rejected blacks' offers of assistance. Patriotic black men who formed their own units were threatened by mobs. This was true in Cincinnati where, as a black leader later recalled:

A meeting of the colored citizens of Cincinnati was called to organize a company of "Home Guards." They did not propose to invade the South, but merely desired to aid in the defense of the city, should the necessity arise. The blood boils with indignation at the remembrance of the insults heaped upon them for this simple offer. The keys of the school-house, in which a second meeting was proposed, were roughly demanded by the police. The proprietor of a place selected as a recruiting station was compelled to take down an American flag which he had raised over his door. The proprietors of another place were told by the police: "We want you d—d niggers to keep out of this; this is a white man's war."

"This is a white man's war!" Everywhere they turned, Northern blacks were told they were second-class citizens and must stay out of a war being fought only to save the Union, not to abolish slavery. Indeed, it was well known that some Northern generals were returning fugitive slaves who had entered Union army camps to their masters. Such developments dampened the enthusiasm of otherwise militant blacks for the Northern war effort. One African-American from Troy, New York wrote:

We have nothing to gain, and everything to lose, by entering the lists as combatants. In the first place the authorities have not called upon us . . . And suppose we were invited, what duty would we then owe to ourselves and our posterity? We are in advance of our fathers [who fought in the American Revolution]. They put confidence in the word of the whites only to feel the dagger of slavery driven deeper into the heart throbbing with emotions of joy for freedom. We are not going to reenact that tragedy. Our enslaved brethren must be made freedmen . . . We of the North must have all rights which white men enjoy; until then we are in no condition to fight under the flag which gives us no protection.

But many blacks were not so easily disheartened. A schoolteacher from Philadelphia argued:

No nation has or ever will be emancipated from slavery . . . but by the sword, wielded too by their own strong arms. It is a foolish idea for us to still be nursing our past grievances . . . when we should as one man grasp the sword . . . We admit all that has or can be said about meanness of this government towards us—we are fully aware that there is no more soul in the present administration on the great moral issues involved in the slavery question and the present war, than has characterized previous administrations; but what of that . . . ?

God will help no one that refuses to help himself . . . If ever colored men plead for rights or fought for liberty, now of all others is the time. The prejudiced white men North or South never will respect us until they are forced to do it by deeds of our own.

The editors of the *Anglo-African*, a weekly newspaper published by blacks in New York City, also came out for black involvement:

There are men among our people who look upon this as the "white man's war," and such men openly say, let them fight it out among themselves. It is their flag, and their constitution which have been dishonored and set at naught . . .

This is a huge fallacy. In proof of which let us ask ourselves some questions . . . What rights have we in the free States? We have the "right to life, liberty and the pursuit of happiness." We have the right to labor, and are secured in the fruits of our labor; we have the right to our wives and our little ones; we have to a large extent the right to educate our children . . .

Are these rights worth the having? If they are then they are worth defending with all our might, and at any cost. It is illogical, unpatriotic, nay mean and unmanly in us to shrink from the defence of these great rights and privileges . . . But some will say that these rights of ours are not assailed by the South. Are they not? What in short is the programme or platform on which the South would have consented to remain in the Union? It was to spread slavery over all the States and territories . . .

Hence, talk as we may, we are concerned in this fight and our fate hangs upon its issues. The South must be subjugated, or we shall be enslaved. In aiding the Federal government in whatever way we can, we are aiding to secure our own liberty; for this war can only end in the subjugation of the North or of the South. We do not affirm that the North is fighting in behalf of the black man's rights, as such—if this was the single issue, we even doubt whether they would fight at all. But circumstances have been so arranged by the decrees of Providence, that in struggling for their own nationality they are forced to defend our rights . . . Let us . . . be on the alert to seize arms and drill as soon as the government shall be willing to accept our services.

But until late in 1862, when the war was more than one-third over, the Union army continued its prewar policy of not accepting black soldiers into the ranks. For the time being, Northern blacks would have to find other ways to aid the Northern war effort.

And they did. A few light-skinned black men "passed" and joined white regiments. Thousands of other civilians worked in the Union army as cooks, laborers and teamsters. In 1861, the Washington correspondent of the *Anglo-African* described the industry of blacks in the capital:

Your readers probably would like to know how the war affects the colored people of Washington. This being the seat of war all classes are benefited by it. Five hundred men find employment each day in the Quartermaster's department . . . Business of every kind for males has increased fully ten per cent. Numbers of our young men [are cooking for] officers' messes . . . Others attend exclusively to the horses of the army officers . . . Barbers and hackmen are doing a thriving business, and the Northern Sutlers' establishments give work to any number as drivers, porters, assistant packers, and salesmen. Many are engaged at the railroad depot unloading and storing the immense amount of freight that daily arrives here from the North and West. Three or four thousand men are employed at cutting wood in Virginia around the different fortifications, and on the northern front of Washington. Laundresses are doing a fine business. They have the exclusive wash of entire regiments and the families of U.S. officers; also for the Hospital inmates. Many females are securing a comfortable livelihood by peddling little notions around the different camps. In a word, we are all doing well as far as employment is concerned. None need be idle.

There were other, more spectacular instances of black civilians aiding the Northern war effort. One of the most famous occurred at sea and involved a steward aboard the Yankee schooner *S. J. Waring.* This account was written by William Wells Brown, a black historian of the Civil War:

In the month of June, 1861, the schooner "S. J. Waring," from New York, bound to South America, was captured on the passage by the rebel privateer "Jeff. Davis," a [Confederate] prize-crew put on board, consisting of a captain, mate, and four seamen; and the vessel set sail for the port of Charleston, S.C. Three of the original crew were retained on board, a German as steersman, a Yankee who was put in irons, and a black man named William Tillman, the steward and cook of the schooner. The latter was put to work at his usual business, and told that he was henceforth the property of the Confederate States, and would be sold, on his arrival at Charleston, as a slave. Night comes on; darkness covers the sea; the vessel is gliding swiftly towards the South; the rebels, one after another, retire to their

*Black workers building a stockade for the Union
army at Alexandria, Virginia* (Library of Congress)

berths; the hour of midnight approaches; all is silent in the cabin; the captain is asleep; the mate, who has charge of the watch, takes his brandy toddy, and reclines upon the quarter-deck. The negro thinks of home and all its endearments: he sees in the dim future chains and slavery.

He resolves, and determines to put the resolution into practice upon the instant. Armed with a heavy club [a hatchet], he proceeds to the captain's room. He strikes the fatal blow: he feels the pulse, and all is still. He next goes to the adjoining room: another blow is struck, and the black man is master of the cabin. Cautiously he ascends to the deck, strikes the mate: the officer is wounded but not killed. He draws his revolver, and calls for help. The crew are aroused: they are hastening to aid their commander. The negro repeats his blows with the heavy club: the rebel falls dead at Tillman's feet. The African seizes the revolver, drives the crew below deck, orders the release of the Yankee, puts the enemy in irons, and proclaims himself master of the vessel.

"The Waring's" head is turned towards New York, with the stars and stripes flying, a fair wind, and she rapidly retraces her steps . . . Five days more, and the "S. J. Waring" arrives in the port of New York, under the command of William Tillman, the negro patriot . . .

The Federal Government awarded to Tillman the sum of six thousand dollars as prize-money for the capture of the schooner.

Steward William Tillman was a civilian; but from the beginning of the war, there were also black sailors fighting in uniform for the cause of the Union. Unlike the army, the United States Navy had never excluded African-Americans, and there had been many black sailors in the prewar navy. Eventually, 10,000 black sailors served in the Union navy during the course of the Civil War.

Thus, in spite of the Union government's refusal to enlist blacks in the army, as early as 1861 and 1862 black men and women were actively contributing to the Northern war effort—and, they hoped, to the eventual freedom of their Southern brothers and sisters. The main Northern objective during these years remained the restoration of

Black and white sailors on the Union gunboat U.S.S.
Hunchback (U.S. Army Military History Institute)

the Union, but the issue of slavery was moving irresistibly to the center of the stage. Northern blacks did all they could to keep the slavery issue in the limelight by urging, day after day and week after week, the emancipation of the slaves.

3

FREEDOM COMES
The Emancipation
Proclamation

President Abraham Lincoln hated slavery, but before the Civil War he believed he had no constitutional power to interfere with the institution in the Southern states. Then, when war broke out, the slaves became the property of the Union's enemies, and as commander in chief of the United States armed forces and with his wartime power to take away the enemy's property, the president now had the right to free the slaves. Still, for political reasons, Lincoln hesitated.

Four slave states—Kentucky, Maryland, Missouri and Delaware—had remained loyal to the Union, and Lincoln feared that hasty action against slavery might drive them into the Confederacy. Also, the president at first hoped that the war would be short and that the Confederate states could quickly be persuaded to return to the Union. Because they would never come voluntarily if the government declared an intention to abolish slavery, Lincoln was reluctant in the early months of the war to do anything that could be interpreted as unfriendly to slavery.

Even as late as August 1862, in a letter to newspaper editor Horace Greeley, who had urged Lincoln to free the slaves, the president stated, "My paramount object *is* to save the Union, and is *not* either to save or destroy slavery . . . What I do about slavery, and the colored race, I do because I believe it helps to save the Union; and what I forbear, I forbear because I do *not* believe it would help to save the Union."

But many in the North, both white and black, thought the Union could not be saved without overthrowing slavery. One of the most articulate abolitionists was Frederick Douglass, an orator and editor who became the most prominent African-American of the Civil War period. A former slave who had escaped North, self-educated and now in a position of eminence, Douglass' words carried weight. From the beginning of the war, he wrote dozens of editorials and speeches asserting that slavery was the cause of the conflict and that victory was impossible without emancipation. After the fall of Fort Sumter, Douglass wrote in his newspaper, *Douglass' Monthly*:

At last our proud Republic is overtaken. Our National Sin has found us out . . . Slavery has done it all . . . We have sown the wind, only to reap the whirlwind . . . Could we write as with lightning, and speak as with the voice of thunder, we should write and cry to the nation, REPENT, BREAK EVERY YOKE, LET THE OPPRESSED GO FREE, FOR HEREIN ALONE IS DELIVERANCE AND SAFETY! . . . Fire must be met with water, darkness with light, and war for the destruction of liberty must be met with war for the destruction of slavery . . . This war with the slaveholders can never be brought to a desirable termination until slavery, the guilty cause of all our national troubles, has been totally and forever abolished.

One of the best arguments of Douglass and other abolitionists was that slavery was a source of strength to the Confederacy. Slaves worked in the fields and factories; slaves dug trenches and drove wagons for the Confederate army. Without their labor, the South would collapse, and the North could win the war. A proclamation of emancipation, said Douglass, would cripple the South by encouraging slaves to flee their masters and come over to the Northern side where freedom awaited them.

The slaveholders . . . boast that the slave population is a grand element of strength, and that it enables them to send and sustain a stronger body of rebels to overthrow the Government that they could otherwise do if the whites were required to perform the labors of cultivation; and in this they are unquestionably in the right, provided the National Government refuses to turn this mighty element of strength into one of weakness . . . Why? Oh! why, in the name of all that is national, does our Government allow its enemies this powerful advantage? . . . The very stomach of this rebellion is the negro in the condition of a slave. Arrest that hoe in the hands of the negro, and you smite rebellion in the very seat of its life . . . The negro is the key of the situation—the pivot upon which the whole rebellion turns . . . Teach the rebels and traitors that the price they are to pay for the attempt to abolish this Government must be the abolition of slavery . . . Henceforth let the war cry be down with treason, and down with slavery, the cause of treason.

As soon as Union forces occupied the border states and invaded the Confederacy, slaves from the surrounding countryside, sensing that the Northern army meant freedom, began to come into Union lines. But, as fugitives, they presented Northern generals with a problem. Should they be returned to their masters under the terms of the Fugitive Slave Law of 1850, or not? Some generals returned them, but in most cases their masters were Confederates and to return property to rebels seemed foolish. The Fugitive Slave Law could hardly be applied to slaveholders who had seceded from the United States.

General Benjamin F. Butler went to the heart of the matter. Butler commanded a Union army base at Fortress Monroe, near Hampton, Virginia. In May 1861 three fugitive slaves who had escaped from a Confederate labor battalion entered the base. Butler, a former lawyer, labeled them "contraband of war" (enemy property subject to seizure) and gave them shelter and work with the Union army. By the end of July, there were almost 1,000 such "contrabands" at Fortress Monroe and many hundreds at other Union camps.

On August 6, the United States Congress passed a Confiscation Act providing for the seizure of all property, including slaves, used "in aid of the rebellion." However, the bill applied only to those slaves who had actually worked on Confederate military fortifications and naval vessels. It did not *emancipate* such slaves—it merely provided for their seizure as enemy property. Nevertheless, it was an important step: In spite of the Lincoln administration's efforts to keep slavery as an issue out of the war, the fugitive contrabands, by their own actions, were making it impossible.

Another way of dealing with the fugitives who flocked to Union lines was tried by General John C. Frémont, a former Republican presidential candidate and now commander of the Union forces in Missouri. On August 30, 1861, he issued a proclamation declaring that the slaves of every Confederate in the state were free. Black people and many white people in the North applauded, but Lincoln was afraid the proclamation would "alarm our Southern Union friends and turn them against us." So, on September 11, the President modified Frémont's order in such a way that it freed only a few slaves in Missouri.

Blacks were disappointed, and some criticized the president bitterly. But Harriet Tubman, the former slave whose secret trips into the South before the war to help other slaves escape had made her the "Moses" of her people, was hopeful that Lincoln would see the light. "God's ahead ob Massa Linkum," she said at the end of 1861, as reported by a white abolitionist in a letter to a friend that tried to capture Tubman's dialect.

God won't let Massa Linkum beat de South till he do de right ting. Massa Linkum he great man, and I'se poor nigger; but dis nigger can tell Massa Linkum how to save de money and de young men. He do it by setting de niggers free. S'pose dar was awful' big snake down dar, on de floor. He bite you. Folks all skeered, cause you die. You send for doctor to cut de bite; but snake he rolled up dar, and while

Contrabands coming into Union lines in Virginia
(Library of Congress)

*doctor dwine it, he bite you agin. De doctor cut out dat bite;
but while he dwine it, de snake he spring up and bite you
agin, and so he keep dwine, till you kill him. Dat's what
Massa Linkum orter know.*

In 1862, the government finally began to attack the
"snake" of slavery. Congress passed a bill to abolish slavery in the territories and a second Confiscation Act declaring all slaves of Confederate masters "forever free" as soon
as they entered Union lines. On April 16, 1862, Congress
abolished slavery in the District of Columbia. The next
day, a black resident of Washington wrote joyfully to a
friend in Baltimore:

*This indeed has been a happy day to me sights have I
witnessed that I never anticipated one of which I will relate
The Chambermaid at Smith's (my former place) . . . is a
slave so this morning I went there to inform her of the
passage of the Bill when I entered The cook and another
Slave woman who has a slave son were talking relative to
the Bill expressing doubts of its passage & when I entered
they perceived that something was ahead and emeadiately
asked me "Whats the news?" The Districts free says I
pulling out the "National Republican" and reading its
editorial when I had finished the chambermaid had left
the room sobbing for joy. The slave woman clapped her
hands and shouted, left the house saying "let me go and tell
my husband that Jesus has done all things well" While the
cook who is free retired to another room to offer thanks for
the blessing sent. Should I not feel glad to see so much
rejoicing around me? Were I a drinker I would get on a
Jolly spree today but as a Christian I can but kneel in
prayer and bless God for the privilege I've enjoyed this
day . . . Would to God that the Law applied also to Baltimore but a little patience and all will be well.*

In the summer of 1862 Lincoln began to think about
issuing an emancipation proclamation. Several reasons
had brought him to this position. His former hope that a
short and easy war would show the Confederates their
mistake and persuade them to return to the Union had not

been fulfilled. Things had been going badly for the Northern armies; they had suffered major defeats at the First Battle of Bull Run in July 1861, the Seven Days' Battles in June and July 1862 and the Second Battle of Bull Run in August 1862. The prospect of weakening the Confederacy and at the same time strengthening the Union by emancipating the slaves and encouraging them to come over to the Union side was thus more attractive now than at the beginning of the war.

The inconsistency of fighting a government based on slavery without striking against slavery was also becoming more obvious each day. The Confederacy hoped to enlist European support for its cause, and Lincoln believed that an emancipation proclamation might discourage England and France from aiding the South, by showing that the North was fighting for liberty as well as Union. Finally, more and more Northerners were becoming convinced—by the deaths of friends and relatives in the war—that slavery was vicious as well as immoral and that emancipation was the best way to win the war and secure a peace based on justice.

But Lincoln did not want to issue his proclamation in the midst of Northern defeat, when it might be interpreted as "our last *shriek* on the retreat." He waited until after the Union victory at the Battle of Antietam on September 17, 1862, and then, on September 22, he issued a preliminary Emancipation Proclamation. The final proclamation came on January 1, 1863. By virtue of his wartime power as commander in chief, the president proclaimed all slaves in the rebellious Southern states "thenceforward, and forever free."

Black people hailed the Emancipation Proclamation with joy. All over the North they held meetings of celebration on that first day of January 1863. One such meeting took place in the Israel Bethel Church in Washington, D.C. The pastor of the church was Henry M. Turner, freeborn black who had migrated from his native South Carolina to Baltimore and finally to Washington. He became a leader in the black community and was eventually elected a bishop in the African Methodist Episcopal Church. He was still living on January 1, 1913, the 50th anniversary of the

Emancipation Proclamation, and at that time he gave his recollections of the events in Washington 50 years earlier.

Seeing such a multitude of people in and around my church, I hurriedly went up to the office of the first paper in which the proclamation of freedom could be printed, known as the "Evening Star," and squeezed myself through the dense crowd that was waiting for the paper. The first sheet run off with the proclamation in it was grabbed for by three of us, but some active young man got possession of it and fled. The next sheet was grabbed for by several, and was torn into tatters. The third sheet from the press was grabbed for by several, but I succeeded in procuring so much of it as contained the proclamation, and off I went for life and death. Down Pennsylvania Avenue I ran as for my life, and when the people saw me coming with the paper in my hand they raised a shouting cheer that was almost deafening. As many as could get around me lifted me to a great platform, and I started to read the proclamation. I had run the best end of a mile, I was out of breath, and could not read. Mr. Hinton, to whom I handed the paper, read it with great force and clearness. While he was reading every kind of demonstration and gesticulation was going on. Men squealed, women fainted, dogs barked, white and colored people shook hands, songs were sung, and by this time cannons began to fire at the navy-yard, and follow in the wake of the roar that had for some time been going on behind the White House . . . Great processions of colored and white men marched to and fro and passed in front of the White House and congratulated President Lincoln on his proclamation. The President came to the window and made responsive bows, and thousands told him, if he would come out of that palace, they would hug him to death . . . It was indeed a time of times, and a half time, nothing like it will ever be seen again in this life.

The proclamation actually freed no slaves: the slaves in the slave states loyal to the Union, and in the portions of the Confederacy under control of the Union army, were not included in Lincoln's proclamation. And it could obviously have no immediate effect in parts of the South still under Confederate control. This led some critics to jeer at the Emancipation Proclamation as a mere scrap of paper. But it was more than that. It was a declaration by the president of the United States that the North was no longer fighting only for Union; it was now fighting for the establishment of a new Union without slavery. The course of the war after January 1, 1863, and the final Northern victory put the proclamation in force, and on January 31, 1865, Congress passed the Thirteenth amendment to the Constitution abolishing slavery *throughout* the United States. President Lincoln played a crucial role in persuading Congress to pass the Thirteenth Amendment. The amendment was ratified by the necessary three-fourths of the states 10 months later.

On February 4, 1865, blacks and whites in Boston celebrated congressional passage of the Thirteenth Amendment at a mass meeting. Several speakers entertained and inspired the crowd, and the celebration ended with the Reverend Mr. Rue, pastor of a Negro Methodist church, singing the hymn "Sound the Loud Timbrel." On the second chorus a few members of the audience seated near the platform began to sing along with Mr. Rue, and in each succeeding chorus more and more of the huge throng joined in, swelling the refrain to triumphant heights of joyfulness. A white member of the audience, William Lloyd Garrison Jr., described the meeting in a letter to his wife:

It was a scene to be remembered—the earnestness of the singer, pouring out his heartfelt praise, the sympathy of the audience, catching the glow & the deep-toned organ blending the thousand voices in harmony. Nothing during the evening brought to my mind so clearly the magnitude of the act we celebrated, its deeply religious as well as moral significance than "Sound the loud timbrel o'er Egypt's dark sea, Jehovah has triumphed, His people are free."

4

"NO MORE AUCTION BLOCK FOR ME"

"**H**is people are free!" How did the slaves in the South accept their freedom? Did they welcome emancipation with joy, or were they sorry to be liberated from their old masters? Did they rush to join the Yankee soldiers, or did they stay on the plantations with their white folks? Did they want the North to win the war, or were they loyal to the South? Did they understand that the war after 1862 was being fought partly over the question of their freedom, or were they ignorant of the issues of conflict?

Some slaves, especially those far from the scene of fighting, had little understanding of what was going on. They remained quietly at home and continued to hoe cotton or tobacco. But most slaves were aware of the issues of the war and their meaning for the future of African-Americans. Thousands of slaves in areas near the Northern army camps left their plantations and went over to the Yankees the first chance they had. This action by slaves "voting with their feet" for freedom forced the Union army to define these escaped slaves as "contrabands." Thus, the slaves themselves took the first step to achieve their freedom. More than half a million of the 3,500,000 slaves in the Confederacy came into Union lines and gained freedom during the war. Many others knew the war might eventually bring them freedom, but they stayed on the plantations anyway and continued to perform their accustomed tasks.

Many years later, one old former slave recalled how, at the end of the war, freedom came to him:

Marse Bob knowed me better'n most the slaves, 'cause I was round the house more. One day he called all the slaves to the yard. He only had sixty-six then, 'cause he had 'vided with his son and daughter when they married. He made a little speech. He said, "I'm going to a war, but I don't think I'll be gone long . . . and I wants everything to go on, just like I was here." . . . Then he said to me, "Andrew, you is old 'nough to be a man and look after things. Take care of Missus and see that none the niggers wants, and try to keep the place going."

We didn't know what the war was 'bout, but Master was gone four years. When Old Missus hear from him, she'd call all the slaves and tell us the news and read us his letters. Little parts of it she wouldn't read. We never heard of him gitting hurt none, but if he had, Old Missus wouldn't tell us, 'cause the niggers used to cry and pray over him all the time. We never heard tell what the war was 'bout.

When Marse Bob come home, he sent for all the slaves. He was sitting in a yard chair, all tuckered out, and shook hands all round, and said he's glad to see us. Then he said, "I got something to tell you. You is just as free as I is. You don't 'long to nobody but yourselves. We went to the war and fought, but the Yankees done whup us, and they say the niggers is free. You can go where you wants to go, or you can stay here, just as you likes." He couldn't help but cry.

The niggers cry and don't know much what Marse Bob means. They is sorry 'bout the freedom, 'cause they don't know where to go, and they's always 'pend on Old Marse to look after them. Three families went to get farms for theyselves, but the rest just stay on for hands on the old place.

But many blacks hated slavery and were more eager for freedom than Marse Bob's slaves. A woman from North

Carolina described an incident that took place on her plantation during the war:

I was scared of Marse Jordan, and all the grown niggers was too, 'cept Leonard and Burrus Allen. Them niggers wasn't scared of nothing. If the devil hisself had come and shook a stick at them, they'd hit him back . . . I was sort of scared of Miss Sally too. When Marse Jordan wasn't round she was sweet and kind, but when he was round she was a yes-sir, yes-sir woman. Everything he told her to do she done. He made her slap Mammy one time 'cause when she passed his coffee she spilled some in the saucer. Miss Sally hit Mammy easy, but Marse Jordan say: "Hit her, Sally, hit the black bitch like she 'zerve to be hit." Then Miss Sally draw back her hand and hit Mammy in the face, pow! Then she went back to her place at the table and play like she eating her breakfast. Then when Marse Jordan leave, she come in the kitchen and put her arms round Mammy and cry, and Mammy pat her on the back, and she cry too. I loved Miss Sally when Marse Jordan wasn't round.

Marse Jordan's two sons went to the war; they went all dressed up in they fighting clothes. Young Marse Jordan was just like Miss Sally, but Marse Gregory was like Marse Jordan, even to the bully way he walk. Young Marse Jordan never come back from the war, but 'twould take more than a bullet to kill Marse Gregory. He too mean to die anyhow 'cause the devil didn't want him and the Lord wouldn't have him.

One day Marse Gregory come home on a furlough. He think he look pretty with his sword clanking and his boots shining. He was a colonel, lieutenant, or something. He was strutting round the yard showing off, when Leonard Allen say under his breath, "Look at that goddam soldier. He fighting to keep us niggers from being free."

'Bout that time Marse Jordan come up. He look at Leonard and say, "What you mumbling 'bout?"

That big Leonard wasn't scared. He say, "I say, 'Look at that goddam soldier. He fighting to keep us niggers from being free.'"

Marse Jordan's face begun to swell. It turned so red that the blood near bust out. He turned to Pappy and told him to go and bring him his shotgun. When Pappy come back, Miss Sally come with him. The tears was streaming down her face. She run up to Marse Jordan and caught his arm. Old Marse flung her off and took the gun from Pappy. He leveled it on Leonard and told him to pull his shirt open. Leonard opened his shirt and stood there big as a black giant, sneering at Old Marse.

Then Miss Sally run up again and stood 'tween that gun and Leonard.

Old Marse yell to Pappy and told him to take that woman out of the way, but nobody ain't moved to touch Miss Sally, and she didn't move neither; she just stood there facing Old Marse. Then Old Marse let down the gun. He reached over and slapped Miss Sally down, then picked up the gun and shot a hole in Leonard's chest big as your fist . . . I was so scared that I run and hid in the stable loft, and even with my eyes shut I could see Leonard laying on the ground with that bloody hole in his chest and that sneer on his black mouth.

One young slave who fled to freedom during the war years was Susie King of Savannah, Georgia. With her uncle she escaped to the Union army lines at Fort Pulaski, Georgia in April 1862. Susie King had secretly learned to read and write while a slave, and during the remainder of the war she worked as a teacher of other freed slaves and as a laundress in the Union camps on the South Carolina Sea Islands. She later recalled that in the early months of the war

[I] had been reading so much about the "Yankees" I was very anxious to see them. The whites would tell their colored people not to go to the Yankees, for they would harness them to carts and make them pull the carts around, in place of horses. I asked grandmother, one day, if this was true. She replied, "Certainly not!" that the white people did not want slaves to go over to the Yankees, and told them these things to frighten them . . . I wanted to see these wonderful "Yankees" so much, as I heard my parents say the Yankee was going to set all the slaves free. Oh, how those people prayed for freedom! I remember, one night, my

grandmother went out into the suburbs of the city to a church meeting, and they were fervently singing this old hymn,—

> *"Yes, we all shall be free,*
> *Yes, we all shall be free,*
> *Yes, we all shall be free,*
> *When the Lord shall appear,"—*

When the police came in and arrested all who were there, saying they were planning freedom, and sang "the Lord," in place of "Yankee," to blind any one who might be listening.

Very early on, in November, 1861, a Union fleet and Northern soldiers captured Port Royal Island and the rest of the South Carolina Sea Islands south of Charleston. Nearly all of the Southern white inhabitants fled to the mainland, leaving behind many rich cotton plantations and more than 8,000 slaves. Soon afterwards, men and women from the North came to the islands to teach the freed slaves to read and write. One of them, Charlotte Forten, a black woman, had many conversations with the freedpeople on the plantation where she taught, and they never tired of telling her how "Massa" ran away when the Yankees came. Harry, the foreman, told how "Massa" had tried to convince his slaves to come with him. When Miss Forten asked Harry why they did not go, he replied:

Oh, Miss, it wasn't 'cause Massa didn't try to 'suade we. He tell we dat de Yankees would shoot we, or would sell we to Cuba, an' do all de wust tings to we, when dey come. "Bery well, Sar," says I. "If I go wid you, I be good as dead. If I stay here, I can't be no wust; so if I got to dead, I might's well dead here as anywhere. So I'll stay here an' wait for de 'dam Yankees.'" Lor, Miss, I knowed he wasn't tellin' de truth all de time.

The legendary Harriet Tubman also came to the Sea Islands, where she served as a nurse and scout for Union forces. One old slave there told her this story:

I'd been yere seventy-three years, workin' for my master widout even a dime wages. I'd worked rain-wet sun dry. I'd worked wid my mouf full of dust, but would not stop to get a drink of water. I'd been shipped, an' starved, an' I was always prayin', "Oh! Lord, come an' delibber us!" All dat time de birds had been flyin', and de rabens had been cryin', and de fish had been sunnin' in de waters. One day I look up, an' I see a big cloud; it didn't come up like as de clouds come out far yonder, but it 'peared to be right ober head. Der was tunders out of bay, an' der was lightnin's. Den I looked down on de water, an' I see, 'peared to me a big house in de water, an' out of de big house came great big eggs, and de good eggs went on trou' de air, an' fell into de fort; an' de bad eggs burst before dey got dar . . . Den I heard 'twas the Yankee ship [the Wabash] firin' out de big eggs, and dey had come to set us free. Den I praise de Lord. He come an' put he little finger in de work, an' de Sesh Buckra [Southern white men] all go; and de birds stop flyin', and de rabens stop cryin', an' when I go to catch a fish to eat wid my rice, dey's no fish dar. De Lord Almighty'd come and frightened 'em all out of de waters. Oh! Praise de Lord! I'd prayed seventy-three years, an' now he's come an' we's all free.

Even before the Yankees came to the Sea Islands, some slaves there had begun to sing the following song, which later became popular among contrabands throughout the South:

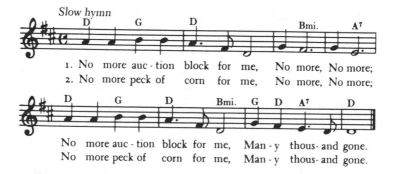

Slow hymn

1. No more auc-tion block for me, No more, No more;
2. No more peck of corn for me, No more, No more;

No more auc-tion block for me, Man-y thous-and gone.
No more peck of corn for me, Man-y thous-and gone.

• 3 •

No more driver's lash for me.

• 4 •

No more pint o' salt for me.

• 5 •

No more hundred lash for me.

• 6 •

No more mistress' call for me.

Many freed slaves flocked to Washington, D.C. during the war. On the evening of December 31, 1862, at a meeting held in one of the contraband camps near Washington to celebrate the issuance of the final Emancipation Proclamation, George Payne, a former slave from Virginia, addressed his fellow freedpeople:

Friends, don't you see de han' of God in dis? Haven't we a right to rejoice? You all know you couldn't have such a meetin' as dis down in Dixie! Dat you all knows. I have a right to rejoice; an' so have you; for we shall be free in jus' about five minutes. Dat's a fact. I shall rejoice that God has placed Mr. Lincum in de president's chair, and dat he wouldn't let de rebels make peace until after dis new year. De Lord has heard de groans of de people, and has come down to deliver! You all knows dat in Dixie you worked de day long, an' never got no satisfacshun. But here, what you make is yourn. I've worked six months; and what I've made is mine! Let me tell you, though, don't be too free! De lazy man can't go to heaven. You must be honest, an' work, an' show dat you is fit to be free; an' de Lord will bless you an' Abrum Lincum. Amen!

Another ex-slave came forward and said:

Onst the time was, dat I cried all night. What's de matter? What's de matter? Matter enough. De nex mornin my child was to be sold, an she was sold, and I neber spec to see her no more till de day ob judgment. Now, no more dat! no more dat! no more dat! Wid my hands agin my breast I was gwine to my work, when de overseer used to whip me along. Now, no more dat! no more dat! no more dat! When I tink what de Lord's done for us, and brot us thro' de trubbles, I feel dat I ought to go inter His service. We'se free now, bress de Lord! Dey can't sell my wife and child any more, bress de Lord! No more dat! no more dat! no more dat, now! Preserdun Lincum have shot de gate!

About the time of the Emancipation Proclamation, many former slaves began to sing a spiritual called "Oh, Freedom." It is still widely sung and became a favorite among civil rights workers in the 1960s.

• 2 •

No more moaning, no more moaning,
No more moaning over me.
And before I'll be a slave,
I'll be buried in my grave,
And go home to my Lord and be free.

• 3 •

No more weeping, etc.

• 4 •

There'll be singing, etc.

The climax of the Civil War was the fall of Richmond to the Union army and President Lincoln's visit to the city on April 4, 1865. T. Morris Chester, the only black reporter for a major Northern newspaper (the Philadelphia Press), entered Richmond soon after its evacuation by the Confederates and wrote the following:

Nothing can exceed the rejoicings of the negroes since the occupation of this city. They declare that they cannot realize the change; though they have long prayed for it, yet it seems impossible that it has come. Old men and women weep and shout for joy, and praise God for their deliverance through means of the Union army . . .

The great event after the capture of the city was the arrival of Pres   nt Lincoln in it . . . There is no describing the scene along the route. The colored population was wild with enthusiasm. Old men thanked God in a very boisterous manner, and old women shouted upon the pavement as high as they had ever done at a religious revival . . .

I visited yesterday several of the slave jails, where men, women, and children were confined, or herded, for the examination of purchasers. The jailers were in all cases slaves, and had been left in undisputed possession of the buildings. The owners, as soon as they were aware that we were coming, opened wide the doors and told the confined inmates they were free. The poor souls could not realize it until they saw the Union army. Even then they thought it must be a pleasant dream, but when they saw Abraham Lincoln they were satisfied that their freedom was perpetual. One enthusiastic old negro woman exclaimed: "I know that I am free, for I have seen Father Abraham and felt him."

When the President returned to the flag-ship of Admiral Porter, in the evening, he was taken from the wharf in a cutter. Just as he pushed off, amid the cheering crowd, another good old colored female shouted out, "Don't drown Massa Abe, for God's Sake!"

The freedmen thanked God as well as Lincoln and the Union army in another song, "Slavery Chain Done Broke at Last."

Jubilantly

Slav - e - ry chain __ done __ broke at last, __
Broke at last, __ Broke at last, __
Slav - e - ry chain __ done __ broke at last, __ Gon - na
praise God till I die.

Chorus

Way up in that val - ley, Pray - in' on my
knees, Tell - in' God a - bout my
trou - bles And to help me if He please.

• 2 •

I did tell Him how I suffer,
In the dungeon and the chain;
And the days I went with head bowed
down,
An' my broken flesh and pain.

CHORUS

• 3 •

I did know my Jesus heard me,
'Cause the spirit spoke to me

An' said, "Rise my chile, your children
An' you too shall be free."
CHORUS

• 4 •

"I done p'int one mighty captain
For to marshall all My hosts;
An' to brig My bleeding ones to Me,
An' not one shall be lost."
CHORUS

• 5 •

Now no more weary trav'lin',
'Cause my Jesus set me free,
An' there's no more auction block for me
Since He give me liberty.
CHORUS

5

WORKING BEHIND THE LINES
South and North

Despite the Emancipation Proclamation and with some exceptions such as the early liberation of the South Carolina Sea Islands, the majority of slaves remained in bondage until the Civil War was over. They raised most of the food for the South and in general contributed to the Confederate war effort. S¹aves worked in Southern factories and on Southern railroads; they dug trenches, built breastworks and cooked food for the Confederate armies; many went to war as body servants to their masters. The Confederate war department actually drafted thousands of slaves to work on fortifications, to evacuate the wounded and carry water in the midst of battle.

Throughout the war many of these blacks deserted to Union lines as soon as they got the chance. The following story was taken down (and shorn of its plantation dialect) by a Northern newspaper reporter from the lips of a slave who had been forced to help load a rebel cannon during the Battle of Bull Run in July 1861:

My name is John Parker, I was born in King and Queen's county Virginia, I do not know my age . . . [When] the war

A slave serving in the camp of Confederate soldiers
(U.S. Army Military History Institute)

broke out, [my master] and his sons went away to the war, leaving an overseer to manage us. In two weeks our overseer also went to the war. We had good times then, and eat up everything we could get. Not long after, our mistress and her two daughters packed up and went off. Our master had told us to stay at the plantation until he came back, and that if any d——d Yankees showed themselves in his absence, to shoot them. Our master had also before this sent us to Winchester and Fredericksburg to work upon the batteries and assist at the trenches . . . Ten of us then went to Richmond and worked for a considerable length of time upon batteries and breastworks on James River. When they were done with us we returned to the farm and found our overseer at home. We worked on smoothly until the excitement about the expected battle at Bull Run arose. They said that all the colored people must come then and fight. I arrived at the Junction two days before the action commenced. They immediately placed me in one of the batteries. There were four colored men in our battery, I don't know how many there were in the others. We opened fire about ten o'clock on the morning of Sunday the 21st; couldn't see the Yankees at all and only fired at random. Sometimes they were concealed in the woods and then we guessed our aim . . . My work was to hand the [cannon] balls and swab out the cannon; in this we took turns. The officers aimed this gun; we fired grape shot. The balls from the Yankee guns fell thick all around. In one battery a shell burst and killed twenty, the rest ran . . . I felt bad all the time, and thought every minute my time would come; I felt so excited that I hardly knew what I was about, and felt worse than dead. We wish to our hearts that the Yankees would whip, and we would have run over to their side but our officers would have shot us if we had made the attempt. I stayed at my place till the order came for all to retreat, then every one ran thinking that the Yankees were also running as fast as we were, they ordered a halt, and the Black Horse Cavalry (which lost a great number in the fight) stopped all the fugitives and turned in pursuit of the United States troops but the general was a little "skittish" about following him, and they didn't care to press forward upon them very sharply . . .

I stayed about here for two weeks, we worked until the next Friday burying the dead—we did not bury the Yankees and our men in the same hole, we generally dug a long hole 8 or 9 feet deep and threw in a hundred in each pit . . .

I then left . . . with six of my master's men to go home . . . When we got back we found all the cattle and mules gone, and corn all grown up with weeds, but we didn't care for that, all we wanted was a chance to escape. There were officers prowling round the neighborhood in search of all the negroes, but we dodged round so smartly, they didn't catch us . . . I was afraid to stay long in the neighborhood for fear of the officers, so I left and came nearer the American lines. I found the U.S. soldiers at Alexandria, who gave me two papers, one for myself and one for my wife; they asked me whether I could get my wife, I said I would try. I then went back, and finding her, I gave her the paper and told her she must try to get off, I told her to come to the Chain Bridge at a certain time and I would meet her, but I found out they wouldn't allow me to pass over there, so I fixed another plan to get my wife over, I was to meet her in a canoe and ferry her across, but I missed her though, and I think she must have gone too high up the river. When I had given her up I went along up the river and came up with some of the pickets in Gen. Banks' [a Northern general] division, near Frederick, Md. I was afraid, but they welcomed me and shouted; "Come on! don't hurt him!" Some of the pickets were on horseback, they gave me a suit of clothes and plenty to eat, and treated me well. They wanted me to stay and go down into Virginia and tell them all about where the batteries were, but I was afraid to try that country again, and said that I was bound for the North, I told them all I knew about the position of the other army, about the powder mill on the Rappahannock river &c. They let me go . . . I left at night and travelled for the [North] star, I was afraid of the Secessionists in Maryland, and I only walked at night. I came to Gettysburg in a week, and I thought when I saw the big barns, that I was in another country . . . I am going from here to New York where I hope to meet my wife, she has two girls with her; one of my boys is with my master, and the other, who is 14 years old, I think was taken to Louisiana. My wife and I are going to travel from New York to Canada.

As the war went on, the South became desperately short of manpower. The Confederate armies were so under-manned that they began to recruit boys under 18 and men over 45. By 1864, a few Southern leaders wanted to draft the slaves as soldiers. The North had been making good use of black soldiers (see Chapters 6–8), and some Southerners wondered why the Confederacy could not do the same. They argued that if the South promised the slave soldiers freedom, as the Yankees were doing, black men would fight as well for the South as they did for the North.

At first the Confederate government refused even to consider the idea. In the fall of 1864, however, the South suffered serious defeats in Georgia, Alabama, Virginia; her resources were diminishing, and she seemed on the verge of collapse. More and more Confederates began to think that defeat could only be avoided by freeing and arming the slaves.

But as late as January 1865 there was still a great deal of opposition to the idea. The Confederacy had, after all, gone to war to *defend* slavery, and the enlistment of slaves as soldiers would be contrary to the cause for which the South was fighting. General Howell Cobb of Georgia wrote on January 8, 1865, that

the proposition to make soldiers of our slaves is the most pernicious idea that has been suggested since the war began . . . My first hour of despondency will be the one in which that policy shall be adopted. You cannot make soldiers of slaves, nor slaves of soldiers . . . The day you make soldiers of them is the beginning of the end of the revolution. If slaves will make good soldiers our whole theory of slavery is wrong.

But General Robert E. Lee, by 1865 the most powerful man in the South, came out in favor of black soldiers:

In my opinion, the negroes, under proper circumstances, will make efficient soldiers. I think we could at least do as

well with them as the enemy and he attaches great impor-
tance to their assistance . . . I think those who are employed
should be freed. It would be neither just nor wise, in my
opinion, to require them to serve as slaves.

Lee's advice was decisive. On March 13, President Jefferson Davis signed the Negro Soldier Law that authorized
the enlistment of slaves as soldiers. But such slaves could
not be emancipated "except by consent of the owners and
of the States in which they may reside." The Negro Soldier
Law was the dying gasp of a crumbling Confederacy. Two
companies of black soldiers were enrolled in Richmond;
but before any full regiments could be organized, Robert
E. Lee had surrendered at Appomattox, and the war was
over.

The freed slaves also made a variety of important contributions to the Northern war effort: they worked as
laborers, teamsters, cooks, carpenters, nurses and spies
for the Union army. The young male slaves were the most
likely to run off to Union lines, and the Yankees were quick
to put them to work.

Indeed, blacks often did the same work for the Union
army that their brothers were doing for the Confederates,
but there was a difference between working for the North
and working for the South. Blacks who labored for the
Confederacy were still slaves, and worked because they
had to. Blacks who worked for the Union forces were free,
and in theory they were paid for their work. Often, though,
so much was deducted from their wages for food, housing
and medical care that they seldom saw a dollar. Racial
prejudice was strong among Union soldiers, who sometimes abused black laborers and treated them in a manner
little different from the way Southern overseers had
treated them. Nevertheless, most of the contrabands who
escaped to freedom in Union lines were glad of their
decision, for they considered even a flawed freedom to be
better than slavery.

Thomas Cole was one escaped slave, however, who
sometimes had second thoughts. He had run away from
his master in Alabama in 1863, and later told what happened to him:

I eats all the nuts and kills a few swamp rabbits and cotches a fish. I builds the fire and goes off 'bout half a mile and hides in the thicket till it burns down to the coals, then bakes me some fish and rabbit. I's shaking all the time, 'fraid I'd get cotched, but I's nearly starve to death. I puts the rest of the fish in my cap and travels on that night by the North Star and hides in a big thicket the next day, and along evening I hears guns shooting. I sure am scared this time, sure 'nough. I's scared to come in and scared to go out, and while I's standing there, I hears two men say, "Stick your hands up, boy. What you doing?" I says, "Uh-uh-uh, I dunno. You ain't gwine take me back to the plantation, is you?" They says, "No. Does you want to fight for the North?" I says I will, 'cause they talks like Northern men. Us walk night and day and gits in General Rosecrans' camp, and they thunk I's the spy from the South. They asks me all sorts of questions and says they'll whip me if I didn't tell them what I's spying 'bout. Finally they 'lieves me and puts me to work helping with the cannons. I feels 'portant then, but I didn't know what was in front of me, or I 'spects I'd run off 'gain.

I helps sot them cannons on this Chickamauga Mountain, in hiding places. I has to go with a man and wait on him and that cannon. First thing I knows—bang! bang! boom!—things has started and guns am shooting faster than you can think, and I looks round for the way to run. But them guns am shooting down the hill in front of me. I tries to dig me a hole and git in it. All this happen right now, and first thing I knows, the man am kicking me and wanting me to holp him keep that cannon loaded. Man, I didn't want no cannon, but I has to help anyway. We fit till dark, and the Rebels got more men than us, so General Rosecrans sends the message to General Woods to come help us out. When the messenger slips off, I sure wish it am me slipping off, but I didn't want to see no General Woods. I just wants to git back to that old plantation and pick more cotton . . .

There was men laying wanting help, wanting water, with blood running out them and the top or sides their heads gone, great big holes in them. I just promises the good Lord if He just let me git out that mess, I wouldn't run off no more, but I didn't know then He wasn't gwine let me out with just that battle. He gwine give me plenty more, but that battle ain't over yet, for next morning the Rebels 'gins shooting and killings lots of our men, and General Woods ain't come, so General Rosecrans orders us to 'treat and didn't have to tell me what he said, neither. The Rebels comes after us, shooting, and we runs off and leaves that cannon what I was with setting on the hill, and I didn't want that thing nohow.

We kept hotfooting till we gits to Chattanooga, and there is where we stops . . . There a long range of hills leading way from Lookout Mountain, nearly to Missionary Ridge . . . They fights the Rebels on Orchard Knob Hill, and I wasn't in that, but I's in the Missionary Ridge battle. We has to come out the timber and run 'cross a strip or opening up the hill. They sure kilt lots our men when we runs 'cross that opening. We runs for all we's worth and uses guns or anything we could. The Rebels turns and runs off, and our soldiers turns the cannons round what we's capture and kilt some of the Rebels with their own guns . . .

I sure wished lots of times I never run off from the plantation. I begs the General not to send me on any more battles, and he says I's the coward and sympathizes with the South. But I tells him I just couldn't stand to see all them men laying there dying and hollering and begging for help and a drink of water and blood everywhere you looks . . .

Finally, the General tells me I can go back to Chattanooga and guard the supplies in camp there and take the wounded soldiers and prisoners. A bunch of men is with me, and we has all we can do. We gits the orders to send supplies to some general, and it my job to help load the wagons or boxcars or boats. A train of wagons leaves sometimes. We gits all them supplies by boat, and Chattanooga am the 'stributing center. When winter comes, everybody rests awhile and waits for spring to open.

Northern generals often got information on the location and size of enemy forces from "intelligent contrabands" who had entered Union lines and could serve as spies. In 1864, the Confederate district attorney of Goochland

County, Virginia wrote that "it is a matter of notoriety in the sections of the Confederacy where raids are frequent that the guides of the enemy are nearly always free negroes and slaves." A year earlier, when the Union army was encamped on the Rappahannock River in Virginia after the Battle of Fredericksburg,

There came into the Union lines a negro from a farm on the other side of the river, known by the name of Dabney, who was found to possess a remarkably clear knowledge of the topography of the whole region; and he was employed as cook and body servant at headquarters. When he first saw our system of army telegraphs, the idea interested him intensely, and he begged the operators to explain the signs to him. They did so, and found that he could [readily] understand and remember the meaning of the various movements . . .

Not long after, his wife, who had come with him, expressed a great anxiety to be allowed to go over to the other side as servant to a "secesh woman," whom General Hooker was about sending over to her friends. The request was granted. Dabney's wife went across the Rappahannock, and in a few days was duly installed as laundress at the headquarters of a prominent rebel General. Dabney, her husband, on the north bank, was soon found to be wonderfully well informed as to all the rebel plans. Within an hour of the time that a movement of any kind was projected, or even discussed, among the rebel generals, Hooker [the Union general] knew all about it. He knew which corps was moving, or about to move, in what direction, how long they had been on the march, and in what force; and all this knowledge came through Dabney, and his reports always turned out to be true.

Yet Dabney was never absent, and never talked with the scouts, and seemed to be always taken up with his duties as cook and groom about headquarters.

How he obtained his information remained for some time a puzzle to the Union officers. At length, upon much solicitation, he unfolded his marvellous secret to one of our officers.

Taking him to a point where a clear view could be obtained of Fredericksburg, he pointed out a little cabin in

the suburbs near the river bank, and asked him if he saw
that clothes-line with clothes hanging on it to dry. "Well,"
said he, "that clothes-line tells me in half an hour just what
goes on at Lee's headquarters. You see my wife over there;
she washes for the officers, and cooks, and waits around,
and as soon as she hears about any movement or anything
going on, she comes down and moves the clothes on that
line so I can understand it in a minute. That there gray
shirt is Longstreet; and when she takes it off, it means he's
gone down about Richmond. That white shirt means Hill;
and when she moves it up to the west end of the line, Hill's
corps has moved up stream. That red one is Stonewall. He's
down on the right now, and if he moves, she will move that
red shirt."

One morning Dabney came in and reported a movement
over there. "But," says he, "it don't amount to any thing.
They're just making believe."

An officer went out to look at the clothes-line telegraph
through his field-glass. There had been quite a shifting
over there among the army flannels. "But how do you know
but there is something in it?"

"Do you see those two blankets pinned together at the
bottom?" said Dabney. "Yes, but what of it?" said the officer.
"Why, that's her way of making a fish-trap; and when she
pins the clothes together that way, it means that Lee is only
trying to draw us into his fish-trap."

As long as the two armies lay watching each other on
opposite banks of the stream, Dabney, with his clothes-line
telegraph, continued to be one of the promptest and most
reliable of General Hooker's scouts.

Slaves sometimes helped the Northern war effort in another way: they gave food, shelter and guidance to Union soldiers who had escaped from Confederate prisons and were trying to find their way back North. One escaped prisoner later said that "it would have been impossible for our men, held as prisoners in the South, to make an escape without the aid of Negroes." The following account by Lieutenant Hannibal Johnson of the Third Maine Infantry is typical.

Johnson was captured during the Battle of the Wilderness in Virginia on May 5, 1864. He was sent to a prison camp near Columbia, South Carolina from which he and three other Union officers escaped on the night of November 20, 1864, by overpowering the guard and running into the woods under cover of darkness. The four men struck out for the Union lines near Knoxville, Tennessee more than 200 miles away. Johnson described the hike in a diary:

Nov. 23 . . . For the past twenty-four hours have had nothing to eat but dry corn which we found in the fields. Must find some trusty negro who will feed us and put us on the right road. At night we approached a negro cabin for the first time; we did it with fear and trembling, but we must have food and help. Found a family of trusty negroes belonging to Colonel Boozier, who gave us a good supper, such as we had not had for many long months . . . Here we remained till nearly morning, when we were taken to the woods and hid there to wait for a guide which these negroes say they would furnish at dark . . .

Nov. 24. Still in the woods, the women coming to us twice during the day to bring us food and inform us that a guide will be ready at dark. God bless the poor slaves. At dark Frank took us seven miles, flanking Lexington Court House, striking the Augusta road five miles above. Traveled all night, making about twenty-two miles.

Nov. 25. Lay in the woods all day, and at night went to William Ford's plantation to get food. Here the negroes could not do enough for us, supplying us with edibles of a nice character . . .

Nov. 28. Still at Ford's . . . About midnight we got a guide by the name of Bob to take us seven miles on the Edgefield road, as the Augusta state road is too public to travel, and some of our officers were captured on that road to-day. Turned over by Bob to a guide by the name of George, who hid us in the woods.

Nov. 29. George has brought us food during the day, and will try to get us a guide to-night. At dark went to the negro quarters, where a nice chicken supper was waiting us . . .

Dec. 2. As soon as daylight the negroes on this place commenced coming to where we were hidden, all having something for us in the way of food; they also promise us a guide for the night. If such kindness will not make one an Abolitionist then his heart must be made of stone. This is on the Mathews place. At dark were taken to the Widow Hardy's plantation, where chickens, etc. were served for our supper. Here Jim took us eight miles, and gave us into the care of Arthur, who, after going with us fifteen miles, gave us to Vance who hid us in the woods . . .

Dec. 5. At dark we were taken four miles, when we found we were going in the wrong direction, retraced our steps, got another guide who took us to Colonel Frazier's . . . The boys on this place were good foragers, for while with them we lived on the fat of the land. At dark December 6th, two of the Frazier servants took us eighteen miles and then gave us into the hands of Ben and Harrison, who took us to Henry Jones' place. Just before we arrived at this plantation it commenced raining and we got as wet as if thrown into the Saluda River. Here we were put into a negro cabin with a fire and bed at our disposal, and took advantage of both . . .

Dec. 9. We were hiding in the woods when it commenced snowing, the first of the season; soon a guide came for us and hid us for the day in a negro cabin. At night some negroes came six miles through the storm to bring us food. We are gaining in strength and weight, for we are eating most of the time when we are not on the road tramping. The snow being so deep it is not safe to travel to-night, so we are hidden in a fodder barn.

After traveling and hiding for another month, Johnson's party finally reached the Union lines near Knoxville on January 5, 1865.

One of the most spectacular instances of slaves helping Union forces occurred in May 1862 and involved Robert Smalls, a slave then living in Charleston, South Carolina. The following account is taken from James M. Guthrie's book, *Camp-Fires of the Afro-American*, published in 1889:

When Fort Sumter was attacked, [Robert Smalls] and his brother John, with their families, resided in Charleston, and saw with sorrow the lowering of its flag, but they were wise enough to think much, while saying little, except among themselves, and hoped for a time to come when they might again live under its Government.

The high-pressure side-wheel steamer Planter, on board which they were employed, Robert as an assistant pilot, and John as a sailor and assistant engineer, was a light-draught vessel, drawing only five feet when heavily ladened, and was very useful to the Confederates in plying around the harbor and among the islands near Charleston . . .

On Monday evening, May 12, 1862, the Planter was lying at her wharf, the Southern, and her officers having finished their duties for the day, went ashore, first giving the usual instructions to Robert Smalls, to see that everything should be in readiness for their trip next morning. They had a valuable lot of freight for Fort Ripley and Fort Sumter, which was to be delivered the next day, but Robert thought to himself that perhaps these forts would not receive the articles after all, except as some of them might be delivered by the propulsion of powder out of Union guns . . . When the officers left the vessel he appeared to be in his usual respectful, attentive, efficient and obedient state of mind. He busied himself immediately to have the fires banked, and everything put shipshape for the night, according to orders.

A little after eight o'clock the wives and children of Robert and John Smalls came on board. As they had sometimes visited the vessel, carrying meals, nothing was thought of this circumstance by the wharf guard, who saw them. Somewhat later a Colored man from the steamer Etowah stepped past him, and joined the crew.

Robert Smalls, for some time, had been contemplating the move which he was now about to make. He had heard that Colored men were being enlisted in the United States service at his old home [Beaufort, S.C., now under Yankee occupation], and that General Hunter was foreshadowing the emancipatory policy, giving kindly treatment to all contraband refugees. Now he was more anxious to get within the Union lines, and to join its forces. He had seen from the pilot-house, at a long distance, the blockading vessels [Union ships blockading the Charleston harbor], and had thought over a plan to reach them with Planter, and his desire was to run her away from the Confederates when she would have a valuable cargo. He had to proceed cautiously in the unfolding of his designs. First his brother was taken into confidence, and he at once approved the project. He, of course, could be trusted to keep the secret. Then the others were approached, gradually, after sounding with various lines the depths of their patriotism . . .

The brave men knew what would be their fate in the event of failure, and so, in talking over the matter together, just before cutting loose, they decided not to be captured alive, but to go down with the ship if the batteries of Castle Pinckney, Forts Moultrie and Sumter, and other guns should be opened upon them. They also determined to use the Planter's guns to repel pursuit and attack, if necessary . . .

After midnight, when the officers ashore were in their soundest and sweetest slumbers, the fires were stirred up and steam raised to a high pressure, and between 3 and 4 o'clock Robert Smalls, the conceiver, leader and manager of this daring scheme, gave orders to "cast off," which was done quietly. To guard against a suspicion of anything being wrong in the movements of the Planter, he backed slowly from the wharf, blew her signal whistles, and seemed to be in no hurry to get away. He proceeded down the harbor, as if making towards Fort Sumter, and about quarter past 4 o'clock passed the frowning fortress, saluting it with loud signals, and then putting on all steam. Her appearance was duly reported to the officer of the day, but as her plying around the harbor, often at early hours, was not a strange occurrence, and she had become a familiar floating figure to the forts, she was not molested; and the heavy guns that easily could have sunk her, remained silent. Passing the lower batteries, also, without molestation, the happy crew, with the greater part of the strain removed from their minds, now jubilantly rigged a white flag that they had prepared for the next emergency, and steered straight on to the Union ships. They were yet in great danger, this time from the hands of friends, who, not knowing anything concerning their escape, and on the lookout to sink at sight torpedo-boats and "rebel-rams," might blow them out of the water before discovering their peaceful flag.

An eye-witness of the Planter's arrival, a member of the Onward's crew, and a war correspondent, gave a good account of it; and with some alterations it is here introduced: "... Well, this morning, about sunrise, I was awakened by the cry of 'All hands to quarters!' and before I could get out, the steward knocked vigorously on my door and called: 'All hands to quarters, sah! de ram am a comin', sah!' I don't recollect of ever dressing myself any quicker, and got out on deck in a hurry. Sure enough, we could see, through the mist and fog, a great black object moving rapidly, and steadily, right at our port quarter ... Springs were bent on, and the Onward was rapidly warping around so as to bring her broadside to bear on the steamer that was still rapidly approaching us; and when the guns were brought to bear, some of the men looked at the Stars and Stripes, and then at the steamer, and muttered 'You ———! if you run into us we will go down with colors flying!' Just as No. 3 port gun was being elevated, some one cried out, 'I see something that looks like a white flag;' and true enough there was something flying on the steamer that would have been white by application of soap and water. As she neared us, we looked in vain for the face of a white man. When they discovered that we would not fire on them, there was a rush of contrabands out on her deck, some dancing, some singing, whistling, jumping; and others stood looking towards Fort Sumter, and muttering all sorts of maledictions against it, and 'de heart of de Souf,' generally. As the steamer came near, and under the stern of the Onward, one of the Colored men stepped forward, and taking off his hat, shouted, 'Good morning, sir! I've brought you some of the old United States guns, sir!'"

Congress granted half the prize money for the *Planter* to Smalls and his men, and later Smalls became a valuable asset to the Union blockade fleet in the south Atlantic. He brought much important information to Union authorities, and during the rest of the war he served as pilot on the *Planter* and other Union vessels operating along the South Carolina coastline. After the war, when freedmen gained the right to vote, Robert Smalls became one of the foremost black political leaders in the South and was

elected to Congress for two terms. Other freedmen, because of their knowledge of the complex waterways of the
south Atlantic coastline, also rendered important service
to the Union navy as pilots and sailors.

But the greatest amount of controversy and glory was
reserved for black soldiers in the Union army. The large-
scale enlistment of black troops by the North was a central
issue of the Civil War, and to it we turn next.

6

"WE ARE COLORED YANKEE SOLDIERS, NOW" The First South Carolina Volunteers

In the first year of the war many Northern blacks had offered their services to the Union government, but their offers had been rejected. African-American leaders nevertheless continued to urge the enlistment of black troops. As Frederick Douglass put it: "Once let the black man get upon his person the brass letters, *U.S.*, let him get an eagle on his button, and a musket on his shoulder and bullets in his pocket, and there is no power on earth which can deny that he has earned the right to citizenship in the United States."

Douglass argued persistently and eloquently for arming the blacks. In August 1861, when the war was more than four months old and the North had yet to win a major victory, Douglass wrote an angry editorial entitled "Fighting Rebels with Only One Hand":

What upon earth is the matter with the American Government and people? . . .
Our Presidents, Governors, Generals and Secretaries are calling, with almost frantic vehemence, for men.—"Men!

Frederick Douglass (Library of Congress)

*men! send us men!" they scream, or the cause of the Union is
gone . . . and yet these very officers, representing the people
and Government, steadily and persistently refuse to receive
the very class of men which have a deeper interest in the defeat
and humiliation of the rebels, than all others . . .*

*Why does the Government reject the negro? Is he not a
man? Can he not wield a sword, fire a gun, march and
countermarch, and obey orders like any other . . . this is no
time to fight with one hand, when both are needed; this is
no time to fight only with your white hand, and allow your
black hand to remain tied . . . While the Government con-
tinues to refuse the aid of colored men, thus alienating
them from the national cause, and giving the rebels the
advantage of them, it will not deserve better fortunes than
it has thus far experienced.—Men in earnest don't fight
with one hand, when they might fight with two, and a man
drowning would not refuse to be saved even by a colored
hand.*

Northern whites first opposed the enlistment of black
troops for two reasons. One was race prejudice. "We don't
want to fight side and side with the nigger," wrote Corporal Felix Brannigan of the Seventy-fourth New York Infantry. "We think we are a too superior race for that." The
second reason was that most people in the North believed
that black men, especially ex-slaves, had been made too
subservient by slavery to become good soldiers. One white
man wrote: "Negroes—plantation negroes, at least—will
never make soldiers in one generation. Five white men
could put a regiment to flight."

President Lincoln summed up both reasons for opposing
black enlistment in two public statements. On August 4,
1862, an Indiana delegation offered the government two
regiments of black men from their state, but the president
said, "To arm the negroes would turn 50,000 bayonets from
the loyal Border States against us that were for us." And
six weeks later Lincoln told another delegation that "if we
were to arm [the blacks], I fear that in a few weeks the
arms would be in the hands of the rebels."

A few Northern generals tried to enlist black troops in
1862, but they were discouraged by the government. Then,

in the last half of 1862, Northern public opinion gradually began to favor the idea of recruiting black soldiers. Union forces had suffered several military defeats in the summer of 1862, and Northern morale dropped sharply. White men had been slow to join the army. Lincoln began to consider seriously the possibility of recruiting black men to supplement declining white manpower. His first idea was to use black soldiers mainly in labor battalions and save the white troops for the actual fighting, but the logic of the situation soon dictated that black soldiers would wield guns as well as shovels.

In the fall of 1862, Lincoln authorized the enlistment of black regiments among the freed slaves on the South Carolina Sea Islands. On November 7, 1862, the first regiment was mustered: the First South Carolina Volunteers. The officers of this and other Negro regiments were Northern white men. Thomas Wentworth Higginson, a famous Massachusetts abolitionist, was appointed colonel of the First South Carolina Volunteers. Higginson kept a diary of his experiences with the regiment; it formed the basis of a book, *Army Life in a Black Regiment*, which was published after the war and became a classic of Civil War literature.

The regiment established its camp on a former cotton plantation. Higginson described the view from his headquarters:

I look out from the broken windows of this forlorn plantation-house, through avenues of great live-oaks, with their hard, shining leaves, and their branches hung with a universal drapery of soft, long moss, like fringe-trees struck with grayness. Below, the sandy soil, scantly covered with coarse grass, bristles with sharp palmettoes and aloes; all the vegetation is stiff, shining, semi-tropical, with nothing soft or delicate in its texture. Numerous plantation-buildings totter around, all slovenly and unattractive, while the interspaces are filled with all manner of wreck and refuse, pigs, fowls, dogs, and omnipresent Ethiopian infancy. All this is the universal Southern panorama; but five minutes' walk beyond the hovels and the live-oaks will bring one to something so un-Southern that the whole Southern coast at this moment trembles at the suggestion of such a thing,—the camp of a regiment of freed slaves.

While the regiment was in basic training, Higginson spent many evenings like the following in camp:

What a life is this I lead! It is a dark, mild, drizzling evening, and as the foggy air breeds sand-flies, so it calls out melodies and strange antics from this mysterious race of grown-up children with whom my lot is cast. All over the camp the lights glimmer in the tents, and as I sit at my desk in the open doorway, there come mingled sounds of stir somewhere in some tent, not an officer's,—a drum throbs far away in another,—wild kildeer-plover flit and wail above us, like the haunting souls of dead slave-masters,—and from a neighboring cook-fire comes the monotonous sound of that strange festival, half pow-wow, half prayer-meeting, which they know only as a "shout" . . . [The soldiers'] hut is now crammed with men, singing at the top of their voices, in one of their quaint, monotonous, endless, negro-Methodist chants, with obscure syllables recurring constantly, and slight variations interwoven, all accompanied with a regular drumming of the feet and clapping of the hands, like castanets. Then the excitement spreads: inside and outside the enclosure men begin to quiver and dance, others join, a circle forms, winding monotonously round someone in the centre; some "heel and toe" tumultuously, others merely tremble and stagger on, others stoop and rise, others whirl, others caper sideways, all keep steadily circling like dervishes; spectators applaud special strokes of skill . . . Suddenly there comes a sort of snap, and the spell breaks, amid general sighing and laughter. And this not rarely and occasionally, but night after night, while in other parts of the camp the soberest prayers and exhortations are proceeding sedately.

One evening Colonel Higginson went for a walk through the camp.

Strolling in the cool moonlight, I was attracted by a brilliant light beneath the trees, and cautiously ap-

proached it. A circle of thirty or forty soldiers sat around a roaring fire, while one old uncle, Cato by name, was narrating an interminable tale, to the insatiable delight of his audience . . . It was a narrative, dramatized to the last degree, of his adventures in escaping from his master to the Union vessels; and even I, who have heard the stories of Harriet Tubman . . . never witnessed such a piece of acting. When I came upon the scene he had just come unexpectedly upon a plantation-house, and, putting a bold face upon it, had walked up to the door.

"Den I go up to de white man, berry humble, and say, would he please gib ole man a mouthful for eat?

"He say he must hab de valeration ob half a dollar.

"Den I look berry sorry, and turn for go away.

"Den he say I might gib him the hatchet I had.

"Den I say" (this in a tragic vein) "dat I must hab dat hatchet for defend myself from de dogs!

"Den he say de Yankee pickets was near by, and I must be very keerful.

"Den I say, 'Good Lord, Mas'r, am dey?'"

Words cannot express the complete dissimulation with which these accents of terror were uttered,—this being precisely the piece of information he wished to obtain . . .

Then he described his reaching the river-side at last, and trying to decide whether certain vessels held friends or foes.

"Den I see guns on board, and sure sartin he Union boat, and I pop my head up. Den I been-a-tink [think] Seceshkey [Secessionists] hab guns too, and my head go down again. Den I hide in de bush till morning. Den I open my bundle, and take ole white shirt and tie him on ole pole and wave him, and ebry time de wind blow, I been-a-tremble, and drap down in de bushes,"—because, being between two fires, he doubted whether friend or foe would see his signal first. And so on, with a succession of tricks beyond Molière, of facts of caution, foresight, patient cunning, which were listened to with infinite gusto and perfect comprehension by every listener.

And all this to a bivouac of negro soldiers, with the brilliant fire lighting up their red trousers and gleaming from their shining black faces,—eyes and teeth all white with tumultuous glee. Overhead, the mighty limbs of a

*great live-oak, with the weird moss swaying in the smoke,
and the high moon gleaming faintly through.*

On another occasion, one of the black soldiers climbed
up on a barrel and gave a rousing patriotic speech to his
comrades:

*He reminded them that he had predicted this war ever
since Frémont's time [the presidential election of 1856], to
which some of the crowd assented; he gave a very intelligent
account of that Presidential campaign, and then described
most impressively the secret anxiety of the slaves in Florida
to know all about President Lincoln's election, and told
how they all refused to work on the fourth of March,
expecting their freedom to date from that day. He finally
brought out one of the few really impressive appeals for the
American flag that I have ever heard. "Our mas'rs dey hab
lib under de flag, dey got dere wealth under it, and ebryting
beautiful for dere chilen. Under it dey hab grind us up, and
put us in dere pocket for money. But de fus' minute dey tink
dat old flag mean freedom for we colored people, dey pull
it right down, and run up de rag ob dere own." (Immense
applause.) "But we'll neber desert de ole flag, boys, neber;
we hab lib under it for eighteen hundred sixty-two years,
and we'll die for it now."*

In January 1863 the regiment marched in dress parade
through Beaufort, the largest town on the Sea Islands.
Higginson described the parade:

*To look back on twenty broad double-ranks of men (for
they marched by platoons),—every polished musket having
a black face beside it, and every face set steadily to the
front,—a regiment of freed slaves marching on into the
future,—it was something to remember; and when they
returned through the same streets, marching by the flank,
with guns at a "support," and each man covering his
file-leader handsomely, the effect on the eye was almost as
fine. The band of the Eighth Maine joined us at the en-
trance of the town, and escorted us in. Sergeant Rivers said
ecstatically afterwards, in describing the affair, "And*

*when dat band wheel in before us, and march on,—my
God! I quit dis world altogeder." I wonder if he pictured to
himself the many dusky regiments, now unformed, which
I seemed to see marching up behind us, gathering shape
out of the dim air.*

Several days later part of the regiment embarked on its
first combat mission, a raid up the St. Marys River (which
forms the boundary between Florida and Georgia) to obtain much-needed lumber and to destroy Confederate
outposts. The soldiers traveled part way on an armed
transport boat, then proceeded on foot by moonlight toward an enemy cavalry camp. As they drew near the camp,

*there was a trampling of feet among the advanced guard
as they came confusedly to a halt, and almost at the same
instant a more ominous sound, as of galloping horses in
the path before us. The moonlight outside the woods gave
that dimness of atmosphere within which is more bewil-
dering than darkness, because the eyes cannot adapt themselves to it so well. Yet I fancied, and others aver, that they
saw the leader of an approaching party mounted on a white
horse and reining up in the pathway; others, again, declare
that he drew a pistol from the holster and took aim; others
heard the words, "Charge in upon them! Surround them!"
But all this was confused by the opening rifle-shots of our
advanced guard, and, as clear observation was impossible,
I made the men fix their bayonets and kneel in the cover on
each side of the pathway, and I saw with delight the brave
fellows, with Sergeant McIntyre at their head, settling
down in the grass as coolly and warily as if wild turkeys
were the only game. Perhaps at the first shot a man fell at
my elbow. I felt it no more than if a tree had fallen,—I was
so busy watching my own men and the enemy, and planning what to do next. Some of our soldiers, misunderstand-
ing the order "Fix bayonets," were actually charging with
them, dashing off into the dim woods, with nothing to
charge at but the vanishing tail of an imaginary horse,—
for we could really see nothing . . .
I could hardly tell whether the fight had lasted ten
minutes or an hour, when, as the enemy's fire had evidently*

*ceased or slackened, I gave the order to cease firing. But it
was very difficult at first to make them desist: the taste of
gunpowder was too intoxicating. One of them was heard to
mutter, indignantly, "Why, de Cunnel order Cease firing,
when de Secesh blazin' away at de rate ob ten dollar a
day?" . . . We did not yet know that we had killed the first
lieutenant of the cavalry, and that our opponents had
retreated to the woods in dismay, without daring to return
to their camp.*

Of the black regiment, one was killed and seven were
wounded in the battle, while the rebel cavalry suffered 12
killed and many wounded. Higginson's men gathered up
their wounded, returned to the boat and the next day
completed their mission by loading a cargo boat with
lumber abandoned by the rebels. As the transport boat
returned downriver on its way home, it came under heavy
fire from Confederate howitzers concealed in the bluffs
along the river. Higginson described what happened:

*Suddenly there swept down from a bluff above us, on the
Georgia side, a mingling of shout and roar and rattle as of
a tornado let loose; and as a storm of bullets came pelting
against the sides of the vessel, and through a window, there
went up a shrill answering shout from our own men. [I
tried to keep the infantry-men below deck, but] after all my
efforts the men had swarmed once more from below, and
already, crowding at both ends of the boat, were loading
and firing with inconceivable rapidity, shouting to each
other, "Nebber gib it up" . . . Meanwhile the officers in
charge of the large guns had their crews in order, and our
shells began to fly over the bluffs . . .*

*We were now gliding past a safe reach of marsh, while
our assailants were riding by cross-paths to attack us at
the next bluff. . . My men were now pretty well imprisoned
below in the hot and crowded hold, and actually fought
each other, the officers afterwards said, for places at the
open portholes, from which to aim. Others implored to be
landed, exclaiming that they "supposed de Cunnel knew
best," but it was "mighty mean" to be shut up down below,
when they might be "fightin' de Secesh in de clar field."*

This clear field, and no favor, was what they thenceforward sighed for. But in such difficult navigation it would have been madness to think of landing, although one daring Rebel actually sprang upon the large boat which we towed astern, where he was shot down by one of our sergeants. This boat was soon after swamped and abandoned, then taken and repaired by the Rebels at a later date, and finally, by a piece of dramatic completeness, was seized by a party of fugitive slaves, who escaped in it to our lines, and some of whom enlisted in my own regiment.

It has always been rather a mystery to me why the Rebels did not fell a few trees across the stream at some of the many sharp angles where we might so easily have been imprisoned. This, however, they did not attempt, and with the skillful pilotage of our trusty [Negro] Corporal,—philosophic as Socrates through all the din, and occasionally relieving his mind by taking a shot with his rifle through the high portholes of the pilot-house,—we glided safely on.

After the men had returned to camp, Corporal Adam Allston described his reactions during the shelling of the boat:

When I heard de bombshell a-screamin' troo de woods like de Judgment Day, I said to myself, "If my head was took off to-night, dey couldn't put my soul in de torments, percept [except] God was my enemy!" And when de rifle-bullets came whizzin' across de deck, I cried aloud, "God help my congregation. Boys, load and fire!"

In his official report of the raid along the St. Marys River, Higginson wrote:

No officer in this regiment now doubts that the key to the successful prosecution of this war lies in the unlimited employment of black troops. Their superiority lies simply in the fact that they know the country, while white troops do not, and, moreover, that they have peculiarities of temperament, position, and motive which belong to them alone. Instead of leaving their homes and families to fight they are fighting for their homes and families . . . It would have been madness to attempt, with the bravest white troops, what I have successfully accomplished with black ones. Everything, even to the piloting of the vessels and the selection of the proper points for cannonading, was done by my own soldiers.

Higginson's men were justifiably proud of their accomplishments. As Corporal Thomas Long, acting as chaplain one Sunday, told his fellow soldiers:

If we hadn't become sojers, all might have gone back as it was before; our freedom might have slipped through de two houses of Congress and President Linkum's four years might have passed by and notin been done for we. But now tings can never go back, because we have showed our energy and our courage and our naturally manhood.

Anoder ting is, suppose you had kept your freedom widout enlisting in dis army; your chilen might have grown up free, and been well cultivated so as to be equal to any business; but it would have been always flung in dere faces—"Your fader never fought for he own freedom"—and what could dey answer? Neber can say that to dis African race any more. Tanks to dis regiment, neber can say dat any more, because we first showed dem we could fight by dere side.

The success of Higginson's black regiment and others organized in the South at the beginning of 1863 convinced the Union government to go ahead with large-scale enlistment of black troops. On April 1, 1863, President Lincoln told Higginson's commanding officer: "I am glad to see the accounts of your colored force at Jacksonville, Florida . . . It is important to the enemy that such a force shall *not* take shape, and grow, and thrive, in the South; and in precisely the same proportion, it is important to us that it shall."

About the same time, Lincoln wrote to a Union commander in Tennessee: "The colored population is the great *available* and yet *unavailed of* force for restoring the Union. The bare sight of 50,000 armed and drilled black soldiers upon the banks of the Mississippi would end the rebellion at once. And who doubts that we can present that sight if we but take hold in earnest?" The president had clearly changed his mind since the previous September.

In 1862 Union forces had captured and occupied New Orleans, a city containing a large number of educated Negroes who had been free all their lives. Their ancestors had been there when France controlled Louisiana, and many still spoke French. They were loyal to the Union and started a newspaper called *L'Union (The Union),* published in both French and English. In the spring of 1863, General N. P. Banks, commander of the Union forces in Louisiana, began to recruit a "Corps d'Afrique" from the black population of the area. *L'Union* came out in support of Banks's efforts with a fighting editorial:

To Arms! It is our duty. The nation counts on the devotion and the courage of its sons. We will not remain deaf to its call; we will not remain indifferent spectators, like strangers who attach no value to the land. We are sons of Louisiana, and when Louisiana calls us we march.

To Arms! It is an honor understood by our fathers who fought on the plains of Chalmette. He who defends his fatherland is the real citizen, and this time we are fighting for the rights of our race . . . We demand justice. And when an organized, numerous, and respectable body which has rendered many services to the nation demands justice— nothing more, but nothing less—the nation cannot refuse.

To Arms! Who would think to save himself by neutrality? Would the enemies of the country and of our race have more respect for those who stand timidly apart than for the brave who look them in the face? In what century and in what land has man made himself respected in wartime by cowardice? The scorn of the conqueror is the reward of weakness.

By the end of August, Banks had recruited nearly 15,000 black soldiers in Louisiana. Meanwhile, the War Department in Washington created a "Bureau of Colored Troops" to supervise the enlistment of Negro soldiers in both North and South.

Wherever the Northern armies penetrated into the south, officers were put to work enlisting freedmen. In

Nashville, occupied by Union forces, the blacks held a recruitment meeting. One former slave, Jerry Sullivan, told the crowd:

God is in this war. He will lead us on to victory. Folks talk about the fighting being nearly over, but I believe there is a heap yet to come. Let the colored men accept the offer of the President and Cabinet, take arms, join the army, and then we will whip the rebels, even if Longstreet and all the Streets of the South, concentrate at Chattanooga. (Laughter and applause.) . . . I ran away two years ago . . . I got to Cincinnati, and from there I went straight to General Rosecrans' headquarters. And now I am going to be Corporal. (Shouts of laughter.)

Come, boys, let's get some guns from Uncle Sam, and go coon hunting; shooting those gray back coons [Confederates] that go poking about the country now a days. (Laughter.) Tomorrow morning, don't eat too much breakfast, but as soon as you get back from market, start the first thing for our camp. Don't ask your wife, for if she is a wife worth having she will call you a coward for asking her. (Applause, and waving of handkerchiefs by the ladies.) I've got a wife and she says to me, the other day, "Jerry, if you don't go to the war mighty soon, I'll go off and leave you, as some of the Northern gentlemen want me to go home to cook for them." (Laughter.) . . . The ladies are now busy making us a flag, and let us prove ourselves men worthy to bear it.

The enthusiasm of newly formed black regiments was frequently expressed in son. A drummer boy in one of the Kentucky black regiments wrote new words for the tune of "Yankee Doodle":

Before and after photographs of a young contra-
band who became a Union drummer boy
(U.S. Army Military History Institute)

swears he's one of Lin - coln's men, He's
cut - ting al - might - y cap - ers.

• 2 •

Captain Fidler's come to town,
With his abolition triggers;
He swears he's one of Lincoln's men,
"Enlisting all the niggers."

• 3 •

You'll see the rebels on the street,
Their noses like a bee gum;
I don't care what in thunder they say,
I'm fighting for my freedom!

• 4 •

My old massa's come to town,
Cutting a Southern figure;
What's the matter with the man?
Lincoln's got his niggers.

• 5 •

We'll get our colored regiments strung
Out in a line of battle;
I'll bet my money agin' the South
The rebels will skedaddle.

"John Brown's Body" was a favorite marching song with all Union troops, black as well as white. One black regiment, the First Arkansas, made up some new words for it:

March tempo

Oh, we're the bul - ly sol - diers of the

"First of Ark-an-sas," We are fight-ing for the U-nion, we are fight-ing for the law, We can hit a re-bel fur-ther than a white man e-ver saw, As we go mar-ching on. Glo-ry Glo-ry Hal-le-lu-jah, Glo-ry Glo-ry Hal-le-lu-jah, Glo-ry Glo-ry Hal-le-lu-jah, His truth is mar-ching on.

• 2 •

See, there above the center, where the
flag is waving bright,
We are going out of slavery; we're bound
for freedom's light;
We mean to show Jeff Davis how the
Africans can fight,
As we go marching on!
CHORUS

• 3 •

We have done with hoeing cotton, we
have done with hoeing
    corn,
We are colored Yankee soldiers, now, as
sure as you are born;

When the masters hear us yelling, they'll
think it's Gabriel's
   horn,
As we go marching on.
        CHORUS

• 4 •

We heard the Proclamation, master
hush it as he will,
The bird he sing it to us, hoppin' on the
cotton hill,
And the possum up the gum tree, he
couldn't keep it still,
As he went climbing on.
        CHORUS

• 5 •

They said, "Now colored brethren, you
shall be forever free,
From the first of January, Eighteen-
hundred-sixty-three."
We heard it in the river going rushing to
the sea,
As it went sounding on.
        CHORUS

• 6 •

Then fall in, colored brethren, you'd bet-
ter do it soon,
Don't you hear the drum a-beating the
Yankee Doodle tune?
We are with you now this morning, we'll
be far away at noon,
As we go marching on.
        CHORUS

Understandably, the response of *Northern* blacks to
Lincoln's call for enlistment was characterized both by
enthusiasm and reserve. The government had taken so
long to call them to the colors that some were no longer
eager to join. They remembered 1861 and wondered if they
could trust the government. And while most non-commis-

sioned officers (corporal and sergeant) of black regiments were to be black, commissioned officers (lieutenant and above) were to be white—excepting only two regiments in New Orleans, whose officers in 1863 were black. Many intelligent and educated Northern blacks resented this policy, but the *Anglo-African* asked black men:

Should we not with two centuries of cruel wrong stirring our heart's blood, be but too willing to embrace any chance to settle accounts with the slaveholders? . . .

Can you ask any more than a chance to drive bayonet or bullet into the slaveholders' hearts? Are you most anxious to be captains and colonels, or to extirpate these vipers from the face of the earth? The government has clothed you with citizenship, and has announced the freedom of all our brethren within the grasp of the rebellion, is there any higher, any nobler duty than to rush into the heart of the South, and pluck out from the grasp of the slaveholders the victims of their lust and tyranny?

Frederick Douglass said privately that "it is a little cruel to say to the black soldier that he shall not rise to be an officer of the United States whatever may be his merits; but I see that though coupled with this disadvantage colored men should hail the opportunity of getting on the United States uniform as a very great advance." Publicly he said:

Shall colored men enlist notwithstanding this unjust and ungenerous barrier raised against them? We answer yes. Go into the army and go with a will and a determination to blot out this and all other mean discriminations against us. To say we won't be soldiers because we cannot be colonels is like saying we won't go into the water till we have learned to swim. A half a loaf is better than no bread—and to go into the army is the speediest and best way to overcome the prejudice which has dictated unjust laws against us. To allow us in the army at all, is a great concession. Let us take this little the better to get more. By showing that we deserve the little is the best way to gain much. Once in the United States uniform and the colored man has a springing board under him by which he can jump to loftier heights.

Shamed or encouraged by such appeals, blacks in the North began signing up. By the beginning of August 1863, there were 14 black regiments in the field or ready for service, and 24 more were in the process of organization. Five of the 14 battle-ready regiments had been recruited in the North.

All did not necessarily go smoothly once a regiment was organized. A black regiment formed in Washington, D.C. found the atmosphere in the capital, with its Southern traditions, at first hostile. Street-corner loafers and bullies liked to beat up blacks in uniform. A city policeman was reported to have said he would put as many bullets through a "nigger" recruit as he would through a mad dog. The Washington correspondent of the *Christian Recorder* (the newspaper of the African Methodist Episcopal Church) reported in June 1863:

Passing along 7th Street, a few evenings ago, I saw an excited rabble pursuing a corporal belonging to the 1st Colored Regiment, District vols., named John Ross. Among the pursuers, was a United States police officer. Ross protested against being dragged away by these ruffians, at the same time expressing his willingness to accompany the police officer to whatever place he might designate; claiming at the same time his (the police officer's) protection from his assailants. But, shameful to say, that officer, after he had arrested Ross, permitted a cowardly villain to violently choke and otherwise maltreat him. After the melee, the corporal received some pretty severe bruises, whether from the policeman's club or from the stones that were thrown by the mob, I will not say. He quietly walked to the central guard house with this conservator of the peace, amidst the clamoring of the mob, their yells and shouts of "Kill the black son of a bitch," etc., etc., "strip him, we'll stop this negro enlistment," etc. etc.

Enlistment continued in spite of these harassments, and by October 1863 there were 58 black regiments in the

Union army with a total strength (including white officers) of 37,482 men. They came from eight Northern states, including Maryland, seven Confederate states and the District of Columbia. Recruitment would expand greatly in 1864, but already in 1863 the policy of black enlistment had proved a success.

7

BLACK GLORY
The Massachusetts
Fifty-fourth Regiment

Colonel Higginson's regiment had fought well in minor skirmishes, but as yet no black troops had engaged in a major battle. The New York *Tribune* could still observe, on May 1, 1863, "Loyal Whites have generally become willing that they [Negroes] should fight, but the great majority have no faith that they will really do so. Many hope they will prove cowards and sneaks—others greatly fear it."

Then, on May 27, 1863, two regiments of Louisiana's Corps d'Afrique took part in an assault on Port Hudson, a Confederate stronghold on the lower Mississippi River. The attack failed, but the blacks fought courageously, advancing over open ground in the face of deadly artillery fire. Historian William Wells Brown wrote this account of the assault:

On the 26th of May, 1863, the wing of the army under Major-Gen. Banks was brought before the rifle-pits and heavy guns of Port Hudson. Night fell—the lovely Southern night . . . The deep-red sun that rose on the next morning indicated that the day would be warm; and, as it advanced, the heat became intense. The earth had been long parched, and the hitherto green verdure had begun to turn yellow. Clouds of dust followed every step and movement of the troops . . .

The black forces consisted of the First Louisiana, under Lieut.-Col. Bassett, and the Third Louisiana, under Col. Nelson. The line-officers of the Third were white; and the regiment was composed mostly of freedmen, many of whose backs still bore the marks of the lash, and whose brave, stout hearts beat high at the thought that the hour had come when they were to meet their proud and unfeeling oppressors. The First was the noted regiment called "The Native Guard" . . . The line-officers of this regiment were all colored, taken from amongst the most wealthy and influential of the free colored people of New Orleans. It was said that not one of them was worth less than twenty-five thousand dollars . . . One of the most efficient officers was Capt. André Callioux, a man whose identity with his race could not be mistaken; for he prided himself on being the blackest man in the Crescent City . . . This regiment petitioned their commander to allow them to occupy the post of danger in the battle, and it was granted . . .

At last the welcome word was given, and our men started. The enemy opened a blistering fire of shell, canister, grape, and musketry . . . At every pace, the column was thinned by the falling dead and wounded . . . No matter how gallantly the men behaved, no matter how bravely they were led, it was not in the course of things that this gallant brigade should take these works by charge. Yet charge after charge was ordered and carried out under all these disasters with Spartan firmness. Six charges in all were made . . . Shells from the rebel guns cut down trees three feet in diameter, and they fell, at one time burying a whole company beneath their branches . . . The last charge was made about one o'clock. At this juncture, Capt. Callioux was seen with his left arm dangling by his side,—for a ball had broken it above the elbow,—while his right hand held his unsheathed sword gleaming in the rays of the sun; and his hoarse, faint voice was heard cheering on his men. A moment more, and the brave and generous Callioux was struck by a shell, and fell far in advance of his company . . .

Seeing it to be a hopeless effort, the taking of these batteries,
the troops were called off. But had they accomplished
anything more than the loss of many of their brave men?
Yes: they had. The self-forgetfulness, the undaunted hero-
ism, and the great endurance of the negro, as exhibited that
day, created a new chapter in American history for the
colored man.

A white officer of engineers who had watched the assault declared afterward that "you have no idea how my
prejudices with regard to negro troops have been dispelled
by the battle the other day. The brigade of negroes behaved
magnificently and fought splendidly; could not have done
better. They are far superior in discipline to the white
troops, and just as brave." And *The New York Times*, which
had at first been skeptical about black troops, now com-
mented that the battle at Port Hudson "settles the question that the negro race can fight . . . It is no longer possible
to doubt the bravery and steadiness of the colored race,
when rightly led."

African-Americans again fought bravely on June 7,
when two regiments of newly recruited freedmen beat
back a Confederate attack on Milliken's Bend, a Union
outpost on the Mississippi above Vicksburg. The blacks
drove the rebels back in such a furious bayonet attack that
even the Confederate commanding general gave them a
somewhat left-handed compliment: "This charge was re-
sisted by the negro portion of the enemy's force with
considerable obstinacy, while the white or true Yankee
portion ran like whipped curs almost as soon as the charge
was ordered." Charles Dana, assistant secretary of war for
the Union, visited Milliken's Bend a few days after the
battle and later wrote, "the bravery of the blacks in the
battle at Milliken's Bend completely revolutionized the
sentiment of the army with regard to the employment of
negro troops. I heard prominent officers who formerly in
private had sneered at the idea of the negroes fighting
express themselves after that as heartily in favor of it."

The most famous black regiment of all was the Massachusetts Fifty-fourth, composed of blacks from Massachusetts and other Northern states. The Fifty-fourth was the

first black regiment recruited in the North, and a great deal of publicity surrounded its organization and fighting record. It was a first-class regiment, containing some of the finest black youth in the North, including two of Frederick Douglass's sons.

Its officers, though white, were sympathetic to the cause of Negro rights. Many of them, such as the colonel in command of the regiment, Robert Gould Shaw, came from abolitionist families. This was the result of a purpose by Governor John Andrew of Massachusetts, who took the lead in organizing this regiment, to secure officers sympathetic to the idea of black regiments—still an unproven experiment when recruiting of the Fifty-fourth began in February 1863. "It will be the first Colored Regiment to be raised in the free states," wrote Andrew to Robert Gould Shaw's father. "Its success or failure will go far to elevate or depress the estimation in which the character of the colored Americans will be held throughout the world."

For officers, Andrew wanted "young men of military experience, of firm antislavery principles, ambitious, superior to a vulgar contempt for color, and having faith in the capacity of colored men for military service." In a word, Andrew wanted Robert Gould Shaw to command the regiment. A captain in a white regiment with a fine combat record, young Shaw was an abolitionist who considered "a Negro army of the greatest importance to our country at this time." Despite his prospects for promotion in his own regiment, Shaw accepted Andrew's offer of the colonelcy of the Fifty-fourth, braving the jeers of some white comrades, because he wanted "to prove that a negro can be made a good soldier." It was a courageous decision that fit the mold of Shaw's character.

Shaw believed in his men, and they believed in themselves. One soldier in the Fifty-fourth wrote a song which expressed the spirit of the regiment:

Fre - mont he told them when the

war it first be - gun, How to save the __ Un - ion

and the way it should be done. But Ken -

tuck - y swore so hard and old Abe he had his fears,

Till ev - 'ry hope was lost but the col - ored vol - un - teers.

Chorus

O, give us a flag, all free with - out a slave,

We'll fight to de - fend it as our fa - thers did so brave.

The gal - lant Comp'-ny "A" will make the reb - els dance,

And we'll stand by the Un - ion if we on - ly have a chance.

• 2 •

McClellan went to Richmond with two
hundred thousand brave;
He said, "keep back the niggers," and the
Union he would save.
Little Mac he had his way—still the
Union is in tears—
Now they call for the help of the colored
volunteers.

CHORUS

• 3 •

Old Jeff says he'll hang us if we dare to
meet him armed,
A very big thing, but we are not at all
alarmed,
For he has first got to catch us before the
way is clear,
And "that is what's the matter with the
colored volunteer."
CHORUS

• 4 •

So rally, boys, rally, let us never mind
the past;
We had a hard road to travel, but our day
is coming fast,
For God is for the right, and we have no
need to fear—
The Union must be saved by the colored
volunteer.
CHORUS

After completing basic training near Boston, the Fifty-
fourth was assigned to active duty in South Carolina. Colonel Shaw wanted a chance for his men to prove their mettle,
and he chafed with impatience at the minor duties to which
the Fifty-fourth was at first assigned. Then, on July 18, 1863,
Shaw's regiment got its chance. Union forces were making
another effort to capture Charleston, but first the Confederate forts surrounding Charleston Harbor had to be destroyed. One of these was Fort Wagner, and on July 18, Shaw
volunteered his regiment to lead the assault on Wagner. A
newspaper reporter described what happened:

*It was a beautiful and calm evening when the troops who
were to form the assaulting column moved out on to the
broad and smooth beach left by the receding tide. The last
rays of the setting sun illuminated the grim walls and
shattered mounds of Wagner with a flood of crimson light,
to soon, alas! to be deeper dyed with the red blood of
struggling men.*

*Our men halted, and formed their ranks upon the beach,
a mile and more away from the deadly breach. Quietly they
stood leaning upon their guns, and awaiting the signal of
attack. There stood, side by side, the hunter of the far West,
the farmer of the North, the stout lumberman from the
forests of Maine, and the black phalanx Massachusetts had
armed and sent to the field . . .*

*Although we had seen many of the famous regiments of
the English, French, and Austrian armies, we were never
more impressed with the fury and majesty of war than
when we looked upon the solid mass of the thousand
[actually six hundred] black men, as they stood, like giant
statues of marble, upon the snow-white sands of the beach,
waiting the order to advance. And little did we think, as
we gazed with admiration upon that splendid column of
four thousand brave men, that ere an hour had passed, half
of them would be swept away, maimed or crushed in the
gathering whirlwind of death! . . .*

*The signal given, our forces advanced rapidly towards
the fort, while our mortars in the rear tossed their bombs
over their heads. The Fifty-fourth Massachusetts led the
attack, supported by the 6th Conn., 48th N.Y., 3rd N.H.,
76th Penn. and the 9th Maine Regiments. Onward swept
the immense mass of men, swiftly and silently, in the dark
shadows of night. Not a flash of light was seen in the
distance! . . . All was still save the footsteps of the soldiers,
which sounded like the roar of the distant surf, as it beats
upon the rock-bound coast.*

*Ah, what is this! The silent and shattered walls of
Wagner, all at once burst forth into a blinding sheet of vivid
light . . . Down came the whirlwind of destruction along
the beach with the swiftness of lightning! How fearfully the
hissing shot, the shrieking bombs, the whistling bars of
iron, and the whispering bullet struck and crushed
through the dense masses of our brave men! I never shall
forget the terrible sound of that awful blast of death, which
swept down, shattered or dead, a thousand of our men. Not
a shot had missed its aim. Every bolt of steel, every globe
of iron and lead, tasted of human blood . . .*

*In a moment the column recovered itself, like a gallant
ship at sea when buried for an instant under an immense*

wave. The ditch is reached; a thousand men leap into it, clamber up the shattered ramparts, and grapple with the foe, which yields and falls back to the rear of the fort. Our men swarm over the walls, bayoneting the desperate rebel cannoneers. Hurrah! the fort is ours!

But now came another blinding blast from concealed guns in the rear of the fort, and our men went down by scores. Now the rebels rally . . . They hurl themselves with fury upon the remnant of our brave band. The struggle is terrific. Our supports hurry up to the aid of their black comrades, but as they reach the ramparts they fire a volley which strikes down many of our men. Fatal mistake! Our men rally once more; but, in spite of an heroic resistance, they are forced back again to the edge of the ditch. Here the brave Shaw, with scores of his black warriors, went down, fighting desperately . . . What fighting, and what fearful carnage! Hand to hand, breast to breast! Here, on this little strip of land, scarce bigger than the human hand, dense masses of men struggled with fury in the darkness; and so fierce was the contest that the sands were reddened and soaked with human gore.

But resistance was vain. The assailants were forced back again to the beach, and the rebels trained their recovered cannon anew upon the retreating survivors. What a fearful night was that, as we gathered up our wounded heroes, and bore them to a place of shelter! And what a mournful morning, as the sun rose with his clear beams, and revealed our terrible losses!

The assault on Fort Wagner was a military failure, but in a broader sense it was a significant triumph for the Massachusetts Fifty-fourth. As the New York *Tribune* later declared:

It is not too much to say that if this Massachusetts Fifty-fourth had faltered when its trial came, two hundred thousand colored troops for whom it was a pioneer would never have been put into the field, or would not have been put in for another year, which would have been equivalent to protracting the war into 1866. But it did not falter. It made Fort Wagner such a name to the colored race as Bunker Hill has been for ninety years to the white Yankees.

When Union forces sent a flag of truce to Fort Wagner after the battle to request the body of Colonel Shaw for a decent burial, the Confederates replied that dead Yankees, white and black, had already been buried in a long trench. The Confederate general was reported to have said contemptuously of Colonel Shaw, "We have buried him with his niggers." This statement sent a wave of anger through the North and became the basis for several poems and songs to inspire black soldiers to fight harder. One poem was this:

> *They buried him with his niggers!*
>   *A wide grave should it be.*
> *They buried more in that shallow trench*
>   *Than human eye could see.*
> *Ay, all the shames and sorrows*
>   *of more than a hundred years*
> *Lie under the weight of that Southern soil*
>   *Despite those cruel sneers.*

It was not only the newspapers and orators who lavished praise upon black soldiers. On August 23, 1863, General Grant penned a private letter to Lincoln:

I have given the subject of arming the negro my hearty support. This, with the emancipation of the negro, is the heavyest blow yet given the Confederacy . . . By arming the negro we have added a powerful ally. They will make good soldiers and taking them from the enemy weakens him in the same proportion they strengthen us. I am therefore most decidedly in favor of pushing this policy to the enlistment of a force sufficient to hold all the South falling into our hands and to aid in capturing more.

Several days later, in a public letter reproving Northern opponents of emancipation and the use of black troops, Lincoln said:

Company E, 4th U.S. Colored Troops (Library of Congress)

Some of the commanders of our armies in the field who have given us our most important successes, believe the emancipation policy, and the use of colored troops, constitute the heaviest blow yet dealt to the rebellion . . . You say you will not fight to free negroes. Some of them seem willing to fight for you . . . [When the war is won] there will be some black men who can remember that, with silent tongue, and clenched teeth, and steady eye, and well-poised bayonet, they have helped mankind on to this great consummation; while, I fear, there will be some white ones, unable to forget that, with malignant heart, and deceitful speech, they have strove to hinder it.

8

"THE QUESTION IS SETTLED; NEGROES WILL FIGHT"

How did the South react to the North's use of black troops? Southerners had always feared slave insurrection, and now the Yankees, by arming former slaves, were encouraging it. The Confederacy's first response was defiant and angry. On May 1, 1863, the Confederate Congress authorized President Jefferson Davis to punish captured white officers of black regiments by death for inciting a slave insurrection. Captured ex-slave soldiers were to be turned over to the government of the state in which they were taken and dealt with according to the law of that state. Since most Southern states imposed the death penalty for insurrection, this could have meant hanging for captured black soldiers.

It was hard to believe that the Confederacy would actually carry out such a barbarous policy, and for the most part the South did *not* officially execute white officers or black soldiers. But in 1863 there were some reports that captured black soldiers had been murdered in cold blood by their captors or sold into slavery. In response, on July 30, 1863, President Lincoln proclaimed that for every Union prisoner executed or mistreated, a rebel prisoner in Northern hands would be treated the same way. After this, there were fewer reports of Southern outrages against black prisoners of war.

But Southern whites were accustomed to looking upon black men as slaves, and it was hard for them to accept the idea that black soldiers were free men who must be treated according to the laws of war, not the laws of slavery. In some instances, rebel officers or soldiers refused to take black prisoners or murdered them after they had surrendered. The "Fort Pillow Massacre" was the most notorious instance of the slaughter of black prisoners.

Fort Pillow was a Union outpost on the Mississippi River, garrisoned by 570 troops, of whom almost half were black. On April 12, 1864, General Nathan Bedford Forrest led a Confederate attack on the fort and captured it. Several dozen Union soldiers, mostly Negroes, were murdered in cold blood after they had surrendered. A congressional committee later questioned 21 black survivors of the massacre. The testimony of three—and the experiences of the others were similar—was as follows:

Sergeant Benjamin Robinson, (colored) company D, 6th United States heavy artillery, sworn and examined . . .
QUESTION. *Were you at Fort Pillow in the fight there?*
ANSWER. *Yes, sir.*
QUESTION. *What did you see there?*
ANSWER. *I saw them shoot two white men right by the side of me after they had laid their guns down. They shot a black man clear over into the river. Then they hallooed to me to come up the hill, and I came up. They said, "Give me your money, you damned nigger." I told him I did not have any. "Give me your money, or I will blow your brains out." Then they told me to lie down, and I laid down, and they stripped everything off me.*
QUESTION. *This was the day of the fight?*
ANSWER. *Yes, sir.*
QUESTION. *Go on. Did they shoot you?*
ANSWER. *Yes, sir. After they stripped me and took my money away from me they dragged me up the hill a little piece, and laid me down flat on my stomach; I laid there till night, and they took me down to an old house, and said*

they would kill me the next morning. I got up and commenced crawling down the hill; I could not walk.

QUESTION. *When were you shot?*

ANSWER. *About 3 o'clock.*

QUESTION. *Before they stripped you?*

ANSWER. *Yes, sir. They shot me before they said, "come up."*

QUESTION. *After you had surrendered?*

ANSWER. *Yes, sir; they shot pretty nearly all of them after they surrendered . . .*

Major Williams, (colored) private, company B, 6th United States heavy artillery, sworn and examined.

By the chairman:

QUESTION. *Where were you raised?*

ANSWER. *In Tennessee and North Mississippi.*

QUESTION. *Where did you enlist?*

ANSWER. *In Memphis . . .*

QUESTION. *Were you in the fight at Fort Pillow?*

ANSWER. *Yes, sir . . .*

QUESTION. *What did you see done there?*

ANSWER. *We fought them right hard during the battle, and killed some of them. After a time they sent in a flag of truce . . .*

QUESTION. *When did you surrender?*

ANSWER. *I did not surrender until they all run.*

QUESTION. *Were you wounded then?*

ANSWER. *Yes, sir; after the surrender . . .*

QUESTION. *Did you have any arms in your hands when they shot you?*

ANSWER. *No, sir; I was an artillery man, and had no arms . . .*

Eli Carlton, (colored) private, company B, 6th United States heavy artillery, sworn and examined.

By the chairman:

QUESTION. *Where were you raised?*

ANSWER. *In East Tennessee.*

QUESTION. *Have you been a slave?*

ANSWER. *Yes, sir . . .*

QUESTION. *Where did you join the army?*

ANSWER. *At Corinth, Mississippi, about a year ago.*

QUESTION. *Were you at Fort Pillow at the time it was taken?*

ANSWER. *Yes, sir.*

QUESTION. *State what happened there.*

ANSWER. *I saw 23 men shot after they surrendered; I made 24; 17 of them laid right around me dead, and 6 below me.*

QUESTION. *Who shot them?*

ANSWER. *The rebels; some white men were killed.*

QUESTION. *How many white men were killed?*

ANSWER. *Three or four.*

QUESTION. *Killed by the privates?*

ANSWER. *Yes, sir; I did not see any officers kill any . . .*

QUESTION. *Were you shot with a musket or a pistol?*

ANSWER. *With a musket. I was hit once on the battle-field before we surrendered. They took me down to a little hospital under the hill. I was in the hospital when they shot me a second time. Some of our privates commenced talking. They said, "Do you fight with these God damned niggers?" they said, "Yes." Then they said, "God damn you, then, we will shoot you," and they shot one of them right down. "They said, I would not kill you, but, God damn you, you fight with these damned niggers, and we will kill you;" and they blew his brains out of his head . . .*

Black soldiers reacted to the Fort Pillow incident with bitterness, and it probably caused them to fight more desperately thereafter, for they feared the consequences of capture. At Memphis, black soldiers were reported to have taken an oath "on their knees" to avenge Fort Pillow. An officer of a black regiment in the Army of the James wrote from a Virginia battlefield in May 1864:

The real fact is, the rebels will not stand against our colored soldiers when there is any chance of their being taken prisoners, for they are conscious of what they justly deserve. Our men went into these works after they were taken, yelling "Fort Pillow!" The enemy well knows what this means, and I will venture the assertion that that piece of infernal brutality enforced by them there has cost the enemy already two men for every one they so inhumanly murdered.

A white soldier in a Pennsylvania regiment fighting in Virginia wrote home that "the Johnnies are not as much afraid of us as they are of the Mokes [black troops]. When they [the black troops] charge they will not take any prisoners, if they can help it. Their cry is, 'Remember Fort Pillow!' Sometimes, in their excitement, they forget what to say, when they catch a man they say: 'Remember what you done to us, way back, down dar!'"

In the last year of the war black soldiers fought in greater numbers and with greater efficiency than ever before. Fifteen Negro regiments served in the Army of the James and 23 in the Army of the Potomac during the massive Union invasion of Virginia in 1864. And black troops participated in every other major Union campaign in 1864–1865, except Sherman's invasion of Georgia.

Fighting was particularly fierce around Petersburg, Virginia in June 1864. Referring to the battles there, Secretary of War Edwin M. Stanton told a newspaper reporter that

The hardest fighting was done by the black troops. The forts they stormed were the worst of all. After the affair was over, General [William F.] Smith went to thank them, and tell them he was proud of their courage and dash. He says they cannot be exceeded as soldiers, and that hereafter he will send them in a difficult place as readily as the best white troops.

On July 30, 1864, near Petersburg, black as well as white regiments were involved in one of the major Union fiascos of the war: the Battle of the Crater. Union soldiers had dug a long underground tunnel to a point directly beneath Confederate lines; there they planted a huge quantity of gunpowder. The plan was to explode the powder and to charge in with several regiments while the rebels were still confused and disorganized by the explosion. If successful, this maneuver might have resulted in a major Union victory, leading to the capture of Richmond and the end of the war.

Black troops were trained to lead the assault, but at the last minute General Grant overruled this plan. As Grant later told a congressional committee:

If we put the colored troops in front . . . and if it should prove a failure, it would then be said, and very properly, that we were shoving those people ahead to get killed because we did not care anything about them. But that could not be said if we put white troops in front.

Thus, white troops led the charge, with black soldiers following in a later wave. But the whole affair was badly bungled. The general in command provided no leadership, and as a consequence his men delayed and moved too sluggishly and without effective direction. This gave the Confederates time to reorganize and counterattack. They poured a murderous rifle and artillery fire on the white Union regiments. When the black troops moved up to attack, they actually had to fight their way through wildly retreating white soldiers to get to rebel lines. After fighting desperately for a few minutes, during which many officers and men were killed, the black regiments also broke and ran to the rear. Although the black soldiers were partly responsible for the defeat at the Crater, they fought as well as could have been expected under the circumstances. One officer of a black regiment wrote:

In regard to the bravery of the colored troops, although I have been in upwards of twenty battles, I never saw so many cases of gallantry. The "crater," where we were halted, was a perfect slaughterpen. Had not "some one blundered," but moved us up at daylight, instead of eight o'clock, we should have been crowned with success, instead of being cut to pieces by a terrific enfilading fire, and finally forced from the field in a panic . . .

I was never under such a terrific fire, and can hardly realize how any escaped alive. Our loss was heavy. In the Twenty-eighth (colored), for instance, commanded by Lieut. Col. Russell (A Bostonian), he lost seven officers out of eleven, and ninety-one men out of two hundred and twenty-four; and the colonel himself was knocked over senseless, for a few minutes, by a slight wound in the head: both his color-sergeants and all his color-guard were killed. Col. Bross, of the Twenty-ninth, was killed outright, and nearly every one of his officers hit. This was nearly equal to Bunker Hill. Col. Ross, of the Thirty-first, lost his leg. The Twenty-eighth, Twenty-ninth, and Thirtieth (colored), all charged over the works; climbing up an earthwork six feet high, then down into a ditch, and up the other side, all the time under the severest fire in front and flank. Not being supported, of course the storming-party fell back. I have seen white troops retreat faster than these blacks did, when in not half so tight a place.

Another major encounter in the Virginia theater in 1864 was the Battle of New Market Heights in September. Thirteen black regiments joined the fray, and 14 officers and soldiers of the regiment won Congressional Medals of Honor for their bravery in the battle.

The Battle of Nashville, on December 15–16, 1864, was a key Union victory in which General George Thomas' Army of the Cumberland destroyed the Confederate Army of Tennessee, commanded by John B. Hood. Thomas J. Morgan, colonel of the Fourteenth U.S. Colored Infantry and commander of a brigade of four black regiments at the Battle of Nashville, gave this account of his troops under fire:

Soon after taking our position in line at Nashville, we were closely besieged by Hood's army; and thus we lay facing each other for two weeks. Hood had suffered so terribly by his defeat under Schofield, at Franklin, that he was in no mood to assault us in our works, and Thomas needed more time to concentrate and reorganize his army, before he could safely take the offensive . . .

About nine o'clock at night December 14th, 1864, I was summoned to General Steedman's headquarters. He told me what the plan of battle was, and said he wished me to open the fight by making a vigourous assault upon Hood's right flank. This, he explained, was to be a feint, intended to betray Hood into the belief that it was the real attack, and to lead him to support his right by weakening his left, where Thomas intended assaulting him in very deed. The General gave me [four black regiments] . . . a provisional brigade of white troops . . . and a section of Artillery . . .

As soon as the fog lifted, the battle began in good earnest. Hood mistook my assault for an attack in force upon his right flank, and weakening his left in order to meet it, gave the coveted opportunity to Thomas, who improved it by assailing Hood's left flank, doubling it up, and capturing a large number of prisoners.

Thus the first day's fight wore away. It had been for us a severe but glorious day. Over three hundred of my command had fallen, but everywhere our army was successful . . . .General Steedman congratulated us, saying his only fear had been that we might fight too hard. We had done all he desired, and more. Colored soldiers had again fought side by side with white troops; they had mingled together in the charge; they had supported each other; they had assisted each other from the field when wounded, and they lay side by side in death. The survivors rejoiced together over a hard fought field, won by a common valor . . .

During that night Hood withdrew his army some two miles, and took up a new line along the crest of some low hills, which he strongly fortified with some improvised breast works and abatis. Soon after our early breakfast, we moved forward over the intervening space. My position was still on the extreme left of our line, and I was especially charged to look well to our flank, to avoid surprise . . .

When the second and final assault was made, the right of my line took part. It was with breathless interest I watched that noble army climb the hill with a steady resolve which nothing but death itself could check. When at length the assaulting column sprang upon the earthworks, and the enemy seeing that further resistance was madness, gave way and began a precipitous retreat, our hearts swelled as only the hearts of soldiers can, and scarcely stopping to cheer or to await orders, we pushed forward and joined in the pursuit, until the darkness and the rain forced a halt . . .

When General Thomas rode over the battle-field and saw the bodies of colored men side by side with the foremost, on the very works of the enemy, he turned to his staff, saying: "Gentlemen, the question is settled; negroes will fight."

By the end of 1864 the Confederacy was uttering its dying gasps. On February 17, 1865, the stronghold of

Battery A, 2nd U.S. Colored Artillery,
which fought at the Battle of Nashville
(Chicago Historical Society)

secession—Charleston, South Carolina—was evacuated by the rebels. The first Union troops to march into the city the next day were men of the Twenty-first U.S. Colored Infantry, followed soon afterward by detachments of the Fifty-fourth and Fifty-fifth Massachusetts (The Fifty-fifth was the second black regiment from Massachusetts). Colonel Charles B. Fox of the Fifty-fifth wrote of his regiment's entry into Charleston:

Words would fail to describe the scene which those who witnessed it will never forget—the welcome given to a regiment of colored troops by their people redeemed from slavery . . . The few white inhabitants left in the town were either alarmed or indignant, and generally remained in their houses; but the colored people turned out en masse . . . Cheers, blessings, prayers, and songs were heard on every side. Men and women crowded to shake hands with men and officers . . .

On through the streets of the rebel city passed the column, on through the chief seat of that slave power, tottering to its fall. Its walls rung to the chorus of manly voices singing "John Brown," "Babylon is Falling," and the "Battle-Cry of Freedom;" while, at intervals, the national airs, long unheard there, were played by the regimental band. The glory and triumph of this hour may be imagined, but can never be described. It was one of those occasions which happen but once in a lifetime, to be lived over in memory for ever.

And the first to enter Richmond, after its evacuation on April 2, were black troopers of the Fifth Massachusetts Cavalry. Close behind them came soldiers from General Godfrey Weitzel's Twenty-fifth Army Corps, an all-Negro corps of 32 regiments.

In all, official records show a total of 178,985 enlisted men and 7,122 officers in black regiments during the Civil War—9% of the Union army. They fought in 449 engagements, of which 39 were major battles. Approximately 37,300 black men lost their lives for the Union; and 17 black soldiers and four sailors were awarded Congressional Medals of Honor.

9

DISCRIMINATION IN THE UNION ARMY

Even as black troops were fighting for their freedom and their country, they also had to struggle for fair treatment and equal rights within the army itself, for black soldiers were often victims of discrimination. African-American regiments were sometimes issued inferior guns and ammunition, and black soldiers were assigned more than their share of heavy labor and fatigue duty.

But the most galling discrimination was the matter of pay. The Massachusetts and South Carolina regiments had enlisted under a War Department promise that they would receive the same pay as white soldiers. However, the only law which applied specifically to black soldiers was the Militia Act of July 17, 1862. It provided that blacks would be paid $10 per month, out of which $3 would be deducted for clothing. White privates received $13 per month *plus* a clothing allowance of $3.50.

At the time the Militia Act was passed, the government had planned to enroll blacks mainly as laborers, not combat soldiers. When Secretary of War Stanton formed the Bureau of Colored Troops in May, 1863, he asked for a ruling on colored soldiers' pay, and was informed that by law their pay was $10 per month. As of June 1863 all black soldiers were paid at this rate—despite the fact that many were giving their lives on the battlefield for the Union.

Negroes were disheartened and angered by this decision. So were their white officers. Colonel Shaw wrote angrily to Governor Andrew that if the Massachusetts Fifty-fourth came under this ruling, they should "be mustered out of the service, as they were enlisted on the understanding that they were to be on the same footing as other Massachusetts volunteers." With Shaw's encouragement, the men of the Fifty-fourth and Fifty-fifth Massachusetts decided not to accept any pay at all until they were treated and paid as equals. It was not merely a case of holding out for higher wages: The point at issue was not an amount but a principle. Second-class status in the army symbolized second-class citizenship in the nation, and black soldiers wanted first-class status as soldiers as a step toward first-class citizenship in postwar America.

A private in the Fifty-fourth Massachusetts wrote to his sister:

Why are we not worth as much as white soldiers? We do the same work they do, and do what they cannot. We fight as well as they do. Have they forgotten James Island? Just let them think of the charge at Fort Wagner, where the colored soldiers were cruelly murdered by the notorious rebels. Why is it that they do not want to give us our pay when they have already witnessed our deeds of courage and bravery? They say we are not United States Soldiers. They want to come around and say we are laborers. If we are laborers, how is it then we do soldiers' duty, such as stand guard, and do picket duty and form a line of battle when the long roll is beat? No, because we are men of color, they are trying to impose upon us.

And a soldier in the Massachusetts Fifty-fifth declared angrily:

We did not come to fight for money, for if we did, we might just as well have accepted the money that was offered us; we came not only to make men of ourselves, but of our other colored brothers at home . . . It is not the money of 1863 that we are looking at! It is the principle: that one that made us men when we enlisted.

One-third of the men in Higginson's regiment also protested against the principle of unequal pay. Higginson wrote:

The best men in the regiment quietly refused to take a dollar's pay, at the reduced price. "We's gib our sogerin' to de Guv'ment, Cunnel," they said, "but we won't 'spise ourselves so much for take de seben dollar." They even made a contemptuous ballad, of which I once caught a snatch.

> *"Ten dollar a month!*
>   *Tree ob dat for clothin'!*
> *Go to Washington*
>   *Fight for Linkum's darter!"*

This "Lincoln's daughter" stood for the Goddess of Liberty, it would seem. They would be true to her, but they would not take the half-pay. This was contrary to my advice, and to that of other officers; but I now think it was wise. Nothing less than this would have called the attention of the American people to this outrageous fraud.

In the 1863–64 session of Congress, the Republicans introduced a bill to equalize the pay of black soldiers. African-Americans expected quick approval, but the Democrats and a considerable element of Northern public opinion opposed it. Democrats argued that to pay blacks the same wages as white soldiers would degrade the white man. The New York *World*, a Democratic paper, declared that "it is unjust in every way to the white soldier to put him on a level with the black."

While the politicians debated, the families of black soldiers were suffering. An officer of the Fifty-fourth Massachusetts wrote in March 1864: "There is Sergeant Swails, a man who has fairly won promotion on the field of battle. While he was doing the work of government in the field, his wife and children were placed in the poorhouse." Even those soldiers who accepted inferior pay found that $10 a month, minus the clothing deduction, was scarcely enough to support their families, especially when they were not paid on time, as was often the case. A soldier in the Eighth U.S. Colored Troops stationed at Jacksonville, Florida wrote in March 1864:

Our families at home are in a suffering condition, and send to their husbands for relief. Where is it to come from? The Government has never offered us a penny since we have been here. I have been from home since the 20th of October, and have not been able to send a penny or a penny's worth to them in that time. My wife and three little children at home are, in a manner, freezing and starving to death. She writes to me for aid, but I have nothing to send her; and, if I wish to answer her letter, I must go to some of our officers to get paper and envelopes.

With all this, they want us to be patriotic and good soldiers; but how can we when we see, in our minds, the agonies of our families? When we lie down to sleep, the pictures of our families are before us, asking for relief from their sufferings. How can men do their duty, with such agony in their minds?

As Congress continued to discuss the equal-pay bill, the mood of the soldiers grew more fierce. In February 1864 a captain in the Fifty-fifth Massachusetts related that "the other day Col. Hartwell received an anonymous letter from one of our men saying that if we were not paid by the 1st of March, the men would stack arms and do no more duty, and that more than half the regiment were of that way of thinking." There was a near-mutiny in the Fifty-fifth later in the year, and one soldier was court-martialed and executed. Officers of the Fifty-fourth were forced to shoot and slightly wound two soldiers who refused to obey orders. More than 20 men of the Fourteenth Rhode Island Heavy Artillery (colored) were thrown in jail. Sergeant William Walker of the Third South Carolina Volunteers, stationed in Jacksonville, marched his company to his captain's tent and ordered them to stack arms and resign from an army that broke its contract with them. Walker was court-martialed and shot for mutiny. This was not the first example in American history of soldiers refusing duty in protest against unequal pay or treatment. Pennsylvania soldiers in the American Revolution had done the same in 1781, finally winning a redress of their grievances.

The protests of black soldiers also achieved eventual success. On June 15, 1864, Congress enacted legislation granting black soldiers equal pay. The law was retroactive to January 1, 1864, for all soldiers, and retroactive to the time of enlistment for those blacks who had been free before the war. Black troops finally received justice in the matter of pay but only after many months of suffering and bitterness.

Black soldiers were victims of another serious injustice as well, one never fully remedied: the denial of officer's commissions to soldiers who had earned promotion. There were two reasons why nearly all officers of black regiments were white men: (1) At first few African-Americans had the experience necessary to serve as officers, and (2) race prejudice was still so strong in the North in 1863 that public opinion strongly opposed the elevation of blacks to officer's rank. As time went on, the first reason disappeared and even the second became less powerful. But the government was still very slow to promote black soldiers.

On July 26, 1864, a meeting of Philadelphia Negroes adopted the following resolutions:

Resolved, That there can be no good reason offered why colored men, especially those who have proved their availability in the field, may not be promoted to command colored troops . . .

Resolved, That our duty to those men, our brethren who are enlisted through our influence, demands that we should not yield this point without an emphatic protest against its injustice to them, and its insulting endorsement of the old dogma of negro inferiority.

Resolved, That considered in the light of official reports from several battle-fields, we have now veteran colored troops, some of them deserving the highest acknowledgments from the nation, and while we battle for the country,

*and continue to swell the ranks of the army, we are deter-
mined to ask for those veterans the same treatment, promotion and emoluments that other veterans receive.*

Despite such appeals, fewer than 100 African-Americans were commissioned during the war, mostly as lieu-
tenants. There were no black officers in the navy.

Still, however largely unsuccessful during the war, the
call for equal rights had been voiced, and the contribution
of black soldiers in helping win the war convinced many
Northern people that blacks deserved to be treated as a
man and an equal. The wartime experience of the 190,000
blacks who served in the Union army and navy contributed to the development of their racial pride and self-re-
spect. Significantly, the blacks' struggle to get fair
treatment from the military began to quicken their drive
for equal rights in civilian life.

10

CIVIL WAR
AND CIVIL RIGHTS

In most parts of the North in 1860, black people did not enjoy equal rights. Five states—Indiana, Illinois, Iowa, California and Oregon—prohibited them from testifying against whites in court. These same states, except California, prohibited black immigration into the state.

Schools, trains, streetcars, hotels and restaurants in the North were mostly segregated, and with few exceptions, blacks were discriminated against in housing and jobs. Discrimination in New England was generally less than elsewhere, but some cities in Connecticut and Rhode Island had segregated schools.

Even in Massachusetts, the most liberal state on racial matters, blacks suffered from prejudice. One prominent Boston African-American, Dr. John Rock, described its effects. Rock was among the best-educated black men of his day. At 37, he had been a schoolteacher, a dentist and a physician, and he was now practicing law in Boston. He could read and speak both French and German and was a graduate of the American Medical College in Philadelphia. In a speech on August 1, 1862, he told a white audience:

The present position of the colored man is a trying one . . . But few seem to comprehend our position in the free States.

The masses seem to think that we are oppressed only in the South. This is a mistake; we are oppressed everywhere in this slavery-cursed land. Massachusetts has a great name, and deserves much credit for what she has done, but the position of colored people in Massachusetts is far from being an enviable one. While colored men have many rights, they have few privileges here. To be sure, we are seldom insulted by passersby, we have the right of suffrage, the free schools and colleges are opened to our children, and from them have come forth young men capable of filling any post of profit or honor. But there is no field for these young men. Their education aggravates their suffering . . . The educated colored man meets, on the one hand, the embittered prejudices of the whites, and on the other the jealousies of his own race . . . You can hardly imagine the humiliation and contempt a colored lad must feel by graduating the first in his class, and then being rejected everywhere else because of his color. . . .

No where in the United States is the colored man of talent appreciated. Even in Boston, which has a great reputation for being anti-slavery, he has no field for his talent. Some persons think that, because we have the right of suffrage, and enjoy the privilege of riding in the [railroad] cars, there is less prejudice here than there is farther South. In some respects this is true, and in others it is not true. We are colonized in Boston. It is five times as difficult to get a house in a good location in Boston as it is in Philadelphia, and it is ten times more difficult for a colored mechanic to get employment than in Charleston. Colored men in business in Massachusetts receive more respect, and less patronage than in any place that I know of. In Boston we are proscribed in some of the eating-houses, many of the hotels, and all the theatres but one . . .

The laboring men who could once be found all along the wharves of Boston, can now be found only about Central wharf, with scarcely encouragement enough to keep soul and body together. You know that the colored man is proscribed in some of the churches, and that this proscription is carried even to the grave-yards. This is Boston—by far the best, or at least the most liberal large city in the United States . . .

We desire to take part in this contest [the Civil War], and when our Government shall see the necessity of using the loyal blacks of the free States, I hope it will have the courage to recognize their manhood. It certainly will not be mean enough to force us to fight for your liberty ... and then leave us when we go home to our respective States to be told that we cannot ride in the cars, that our children cannot go to the public schools, that we cannot vote . . .We ask for our rights.

The Civil War would bring significant changes in the status of Northern blacks, but things got worse before they got better. The working-class whites of Northern cities, especially immigrants from Ireland, were very hostile toward blacks. Their hostility was intensified during the first two years of the war by competition for jobs between African-Americans and Irish-Americans, by the use of black workers as strikebreakers in a few instances and by white laborers' fears that emancipation would bring a horde of free blacks up from the South to take away white men's jobs. There were several serious race riots in Northern cities in 1862 and 1863 in which white mobs murdered many African-Americans.

The worst violence occurred in the Draft Riots in New York City between July 13 and July 16, 1863. In the spring of 1863, the Union Congress had passed a draft law which provided that any man with enough money could hire a substitute to go to war in his place. Naturally, this bore hardest on the poor, such as Irish-Americans in New York City. Workingmen, including Irish-Americans, also strongly opposed being drafted into a war to fight to free the hated "niggers," who would then come North to take away their jobs and compete with them for "social equality." When the draft office opened in New York in July, a mob of white workingmen burned it down and began a four-day carnival of rioting and bloodshed.

The city's black population became targets of the rioters. Dozens of blacks were murdered or injured. Hundreds were made homeless. The Colored Orphan Asylum was burned to the ground. A Negro writer described the riots:

Nowhere did the fury of the mob flame more furiously than in the abodes of Negroes. Restaurants and hotels and other places where this unhappy people were employed were visited with fell destruction. The furniture and table-ware were destroyed, while the Negroes were driven before a storm of oaths, bludgeons, and brickbats. From place to place where Negroes were known to be employed the mob swayed and swaggered with increasing insolence and cruelty. Negroes were constrained to run for their lives, leap into the river, and cast themselves from their hiding-places on roofs of houses. A Negro residing in Carmine Street was seized by a mob of above four hundred persons as he was leaving his stables on Clarkson Street. He was beaten and kicked upon the ground until life was almost extinct; he was then hung upon a tree, and a fire was built under him, which revived his consciousness, while the smoke strangled him.

In the afternoon an up-town mob was destroying every building where Negroes were known to be employed. In the midst of their diabolical work some human fiend cried, "To the Colored Orphan Asylum!" Celtic malice and religious intolerance led the way with frantic glee. The asylum was a handsome and substantial structure, having been erected in 1858. It was located on Fifth Avenue, between Forty-third and Forty-fourth Streets, and gave shelter to nearly eight hundred children. The mob fell upon this building with fury untempered by mercy. The rooms were sacked, the spoils thrown out to a multitude of Irishwomen, who, amid wild cheers, bore them away in triumph. The inmates were beaten most cruelly, and even the little children were kicked and ruthlessly trampled upon. To crown this inhuman crime, arson was added to murder, and the building was fired.

The Brooklyn correspondent of the *Christian Recorder* reported:

Many men were killed and thrown into rivers, a great number hung to trees and lamp-posts, numbers shot down; no black person could show their heads but what they were hunted like wolves. These scenes continued for four days.

Hundreds of our people are in station houses, in the woods, and on Blackwell's island. Over three thousand are to-day homeless and destitute, without means of support for their families. It is truly a day of distress to our race in this section. In Brooklyn we have not had any great trouble, but many of our people have been compelled to leave their houses and flee for refuge. The Irish have become so brutish, that it is unsafe for families to live near them, and while I write, there are many now in the stations and country hiding from violence . . .

In Weeksville and Flatbush, the colored men who had manhood in them armed themselves, and threw out their pickets every day and night, determined to die defending their homes. Hundreds fled there from New York . . . The mob spirit seemed to have run in every direction, and every little village catches the rebellious spirit. One instance is worthy of note. In the village of Flushing, the colored people went to the Catholic priest and told him that they were peaceable men doing no harm to any one, and that the Irish had threatened to mob them, but if they did, they would burn two Irish houses for every one of theirs, and would kill two Irish men for every colored man killed by them. They were not mobbed, and so in every place where they were prepared they escaped being mobbed. Most of the colored men in Brooklyn who remained in the city were armed daily for self-defense.

But the Draft Riots, though terrible and depressing, were the darkness that came before dawn. The sufferings of black people aroused a great deal of Northern sympathy and pushed forward the cause of civil rights. Moreover, the courage of black troops was winning new respect for their race. A government commission investigating the condition of freedmen reported in May 1864 that:

the whites have changed, and are still rapidly changing, their opinion of the negro. And the negro, in his new condition as freedman, is himself, to some extent, a changed being. No one circumstance has tended so much to these results as the display of manhood in negro soldiers. Though there are higher qualities than strength and physical courage, yet, in our present state of civilization, there are no qualities which command from the masses more respect.

A white abolitionist, Lydia Maria Child, told of this incident in the spring of 1864:

Capt. Wade, of the U.S. Navy, who bought a house for his wife in this town [Wayland, Mass.], has been a bitter pro-slavery man, violent and vulgar in his talk against abolitionists and "niggers." Two years ago, he was for having us mobbed because we advocated emancipating and arming the slaves. He has been serving in the vicinity of N. Orleans, and has come home on a furlough, an outspoken abolitionist . . . A few days ago, he was going in the [train] from Boston to Roxbury, when a colored soldier entered the car. Attempting to seat himself, he was repulsed by a white man, who rudely exclaimed, "I'm not going to ride with niggers." Capt. Wade, who sat a few seats further forward, rose up, in all the gilded glory of his naval uniform, and called out, "Come here, my good fellow! I've been fighting along side of people of your color, and glad enough I was to have 'em by my side. Come and sit by me." Two years ago, I would not have believed such a thing possible of him.

At the national level, under the leadership of Senator Charles Sumner, Congress passed several laws against discrimination. In 1862, the Senate repealed an 1825 statute barring black persons from carrying the mail. Democrats killed the bill in the House, but it eventually passed and became law on March 3, 1865. In 1862, Congress decreed that District of Columbia courts could not exclude witnesses because of race, and in 1864 the law was broadened to cover all federal courts.

It was during the Civil War that Congress first admitted blacks to its visitors' galleries. And on New Year's Day 1864, also for the first time, black people were welcomed to the president's public reception and then to the inaugural reception on March 4, 1865. In February 1865 Charles Sumner presented Boston lawyer John Rock as a candidate to argue cases before the United States Supreme Court. Chief Justice Salmon P. Chase swore Rock in, making him the first Negro ever to be accredited as a Supreme Court lawyer. The event symbolized a great revolution since the Dred Scott decision of 1857, when the Supreme Court had denied the citizenship of black people.

In several states African-Americans actively opposed legal discrimination. Illinois had a code of "black laws," prohibiting black testimony against whites in court and forbidding blacks to immigrate into Illinois. In 1864, Chicago blacks under the leadership of John Jones, a wealthy black man, formed a "Repeal Association." The association circulated petitions calling for the repeal of the black laws; and John Jones, who had taught himself to read and write and had originally come to Chicago in 1845 with $3.50 in his pocket, went to Springfield and addressed a legislative committee:

We, the colored people of Illinois, charge upon that enactment, and lay at the doors of those who enacted it, our present degraded condition in this our great State. Every other nation, kindred and tongue have prospered and gained property, and are recognized as a part of the great Commonwealth, with the exception of our own: we have been treated as strangers in the land of our birth . . . To-day a colored man cannot buy a burying-lot in the city of Chicago for his own use. All of this grows out of the proscriptive laws of this State, against our poor, unfortunate colored people. And, more than this, the cruel treatment that we receive daily at the hands of a portion of your foreign population, is all based upon these enactments . . . They think we have no rights which white men are bound to respect, and according to your laws they think right. Then, fellow-citizens, in the name of the great Republic, and all that is dear to a man in this life, erase those nefarious and unnecessary laws, and give us your protection, and treat us as you treat other citizens of the State. We ask only even handed justice, and all of our wrongs will be at an end by virtue of that act. May God in His goodness assist you to do the right. Will you do it?

The contribution of black soldiers to Union victory had produced a favorable climate for Jones' appeal, and in February the legislature did repeal the black laws. Other Northern states with similar laws followed suit during or shortly after the war.

While legal barriers were falling throughout the North, other forms of discrimination proved more resistant. Philadelphia, with the largest black population in the North, was one of the most rigidly segregated cities in the United States. Most of its horsedrawn streetcars allowed blacks to ride only on the front platform; some refused to admit black people at all. Then in 1859, under the leadership of William Still, a prosperous black coal merchant, Philadelphia blacks mounted an attack on streetcar segregation. Still circulated petitions, wrote letters to newspapers and worked to obtain the support of Philadelphia's foremost white citizens. By 1864 streetcar segregation had become a major issue.

That year the Rev. William J. Alston, rector of St. Thomas' Episcopal Church (colored), wrote a letter to the city's largest newspaper:

TO THE CHRISTIAN PUBLIC OF PHILADELPHIA

Within the past week, my only living child having been at death's door, by our physician we were directed to take him over the Delaware river as often as convenient. On our return to the Philadelphia side, on one occasion, the child became completely prostrated . . . Such a deathlike appearance came over him, I felt the necessity of reaching home as soon as possible, and to my satisfaction (for the time being), I saw one of the Lombard and South street cars approaching, which I hailed, and was in the act of entering, when the conductor arrested my progress by informing me that I could not enter—being colored. I referred him to the condition of my child, but all to no purpose; he ordered the driver to go on, regardless of our humble plea . . . Had the cars been overloaded, that would have been excuse sufficient; but the fact of the case is, that the only persons on the cars referred to were the conductor and the driver . . .

Is it humane to exclude respectable colored citizens from your street cars, when so many of our brave and vigorous young men have been and are enlisting, to take part in this heaven-ordained slavery extermination, many of whom had performed commendable service in our army and navy—in the former of which your humble subscriber has two brawny-armed and battle-tried brothers? Finally, we ask, is it in accordance with Christian civilization to thrust out of your street car the dying child of an humble servant of Christ, in whose congregation there exists an active auxiliary to the Pennsylvania branch of the Women's Sanitary Committee of the United States?

Angry blacks held a mass meeting five days after the letter was published and pledged to "employ all just and lawful means to agitate the public mind, that a righteous public sentiment may exist on this subject." The publicity campaign continued, and in 1867, two years after the war, finally achieved success: the Pennsylvania legislature passed a law prohibiting segregation in transportation facilities throughout the state.

Most horsecar lines in the national capital also were segregated during the war. A bill to end streetcar discrimination there was introduced by Senator Charles Sumner and was passed in March 1865. In an effort to test the law, Sojourner Truth, the fearless ex-slave, abolitionist and advocate of women's rights, who was now working among the freedpeople in Arlington, rode the streetcars of several lines. Truth claimed to be over 80, but she had all the spirit of youth and was stubborn to boot. Her biographer tells the story of her rides on Washington streetcars:

Not long after [passage of the law], Sojourner, having occasion to ride, signaled the car, but neither conductor nor driver noticed her. Soon another followed, and she raised her hand again, but they also turned away. She then gave three tremendous yelps, "I want to ride! I want to ride!! I WANT TO RIDE!!!" Consternation seized the passing crowd—people, carriages, go-carts of every description stood still. The car was effectually blocked up, and before it could move on, Sojourner had jumped aboard. Then there arose a great shout from the crowd, "Ha! ha! ha! She

*has beaten him," &c. The angry conductor told her to go
forward where the horses were, or he would put her out.
Quietly seating herself, she informed him that she was a
passenger. "Go forward where the horses are, or I will
throw you out," said he in a menacing voice. She told him
that she was neither a Marylander nor a Virginian to fear
his threats; but was from the Empire State of New York,
and knew the laws as well as he did.*

*Several soldiers were in the car, and when other passen-
gers came in, they related the circumstances and said, "You
ought to have heard that old woman talk to the conductor."
Sojourner rode farther than she needed to go; for a ride was
so rare a privilege that she determined to make the most of
it. She left the car feeling very happy, and said, "Bless God!
I have had a ride"* . . .

*Mrs. Laura Haviland, a widely known philanthropist,
spent several months in the same hospital where [So-
journer worked] and sometimes went about the city with
Sojourner to procure necessaries for the invalids. Returning one day, being much fatigued, Mrs. Haviland proposed
to take a car* . . . *"A man coming out as we were going into
the next car [Sojourner recalled], asked the conductor if
'niggers were allowed to ride.' The conductor grabbed me
by the shoulder and jerking me around, ordered me to get
out* . . . *and giving me another push slammed me against
the door. I told him I would let him know whether he could
shove me about like a dog, and said to Mrs. Haviland, 'Take
the number of this car.'*

*"At this, the man looked alarmed, and gave us no more
trouble. When we arrived at the hospital, the surgeons
were called in to examine my shoulder and found that a
bone was misplaced. I complained to the president of the
road, who advised me to arrest the man for assault and
battery. The [Freedmen's] Bureau furnished me a lawyer,
and the fellow lost his situation. It created a great sen-
sation, and before the trial was ended, the inside of the
cars looked like pepper and salt* . . . *A little circumstance
will show how great a change a few weeks had produced:
a lady saw some colored women looking wistfully toward
the car, when the conductor, halting, said, 'Walk in,
ladies.'"*

During the war Northern blacks also stepped up their drive for improved and integrated public schools. In 1861, five New England cities still had segregated public schools: Hartford and New Haven in Connecticut and Providence, Newport and Bristol in Rhode Island. As early as 1857, Rhode Island blacks began a campaign for desegregation. Led by George T. Downing, a successful Newport businessman and crusader for racial justice whose children had been refused admission to white public schools, blacks began sending petitions to school boards, city councils and the state legislature. In 1864, the drive seemed to be on the verge of success. Then the legislature narrowly defeated a desegregation law. By 1865 politicians were prepared to pass a compromise measure that would guarantee African-Americans equal facilities in separate schools. But black leaders would have none of it, and Downing sent a petition to the governor:

Honored Sir: The anxiety of a father, who loves his seven children, is my apology for personally addressing you. You are soon to decide whether the rights and feelings of my God-given little ones shall be cared for in law. You are soon to decide whether they shall grow up in your midst with manly and untrammeled, or with depressed, dejected feelings. A great responsibility is involved. I . . . entreat you not to regard the unholy prejudice against color which was triumphant when slavery was triumphant,—which should die with slavery. Disregard it; do in the matter, what your heart and head tell you is just . . .

Should any local authority in the State be allowed to discriminate between us and other citizens in the matter of education because of our color, simply to gratify a prejudice which existed to favor slavery? This is the question . . . The Government at Washington; the Western States, which have been disgraced with black laws on their statute books, are repealing them rapidly. Rhode Island is free from this disgrace; shall it now as the proposition of the majority proposes, blot her fair name by enacting for the first time in her history, a pro-slavery, black law, making a distinction among its citizens?

This petition helped defeat the compromise measure, and in 1866 Rhode Island finally outlawed school segregation. Connecticut followed in 1868, and public schools in Chicago and scattered places elsewhere in the North began to desegregate during or soon after the war.

The progress made in wartime paved the way for later advances in civil rights. In 1865 Massachusetts passed a law forbidding the exclusion of blacks from restaurants, hotels or theaters. Several other Northern states adopted similar legislation in the decades after the war. Within 30 years public school segregation had been prohibited by law in most parts of the North. But these laws did little to alleviate the deeper roots of poverty, discrimination and residential segregation that persisted in the North as well as the South.

11

PETITIONING FOR THE BALLOT

The right to vote is a basic right of citizenship. But at the beginning of the Civil War blacks could vote on equal terms with whites in only five states. These were Maine, New Hampshire, Vermont, Massachusetts and Rhode Island, and they had only seven percent of the *Northern* black population. (No Southern states, of course, allowed blacks to vote.) African-Americans in the North had long been demanding the ballot, and they stepped up their demands during the war. Black leaders in the South also added their voices, declaring that freedom would not be complete without all the rights of citizenship.

In Louisiana the right to vote became a major issue as early as 1864. The Union army was occupying New Orleans and most of southern Louisiana, when President Lincoln ordered General N. P. Banks, commander of the Northern forces, to hold an election of state officials and a constitutional convention to reestablish loyal government in Louisiana. Educated free blacks in New Orleans, who had founded the newspaper *L'Union* two years earlier, decided that the time was ripe to demand equal voting rights in the new constitution. *L'Union* argued:

From the day that bayonets were placed in the hands of the blacks . . . the Negro became a citizen of the United States. Schools have been established for the instruction of freedmen, and all reports say that they have learned to read and write so rapidly that the black sergeants, after three months' study, have mastered their books as well as the most pure Caucasians placed in the same circumstances . . . How does one explain, then, the hesitancy of the American people to grant the right to vote to these black men, who have as much intelligence, energy, and vigor as the average white man and much more patriotism than the traitors who have dared to place their bloodstained hands on the federal Constitution? This war has broken the chains of the slave, and it is written in the heavens that from this war shall grow the seeds of the political enfranchisement of the oppressed race.

New Orleans blacks decided to take their case directly to the national government. On January 5, 1864, they drew up a petition for the right to vote and addressed it to both President Lincoln and Congress. It was signed by more than 1,000 men, 27 of whom had fought under Andrew Jackson against the British at the Battle of New Orleans in 1815. Many other signers had fought for the Union army in the Civil War. Jean Baptiste Roudanez and Arnold Bertonneau carried the petition to Washington.

President Lincoln was impressed. The following day he wrote the governor of Louisiana, who was preparing for the constitutional convention: "I barely suggest for your private consideration, whether some of the colored people may not be let in [to the suffrage]—as, for instance, the very intelligent, and especially those who have fought gallantly in our ranks." But Louisiana's new constitution did not grant the ballot to black men: Race prejudice and the belief that Negroes, though free, were still too ignorant to exercise the rights of citizenship proved too strong.

That October, black delegates from 18 states, including seven slave states, met in Syracuse, New York for a National Convention of Colored Citizens of the United States. The convention passed resolutions calling for equal rights and justice in the reconstruction of the Union and issued an "Address to the People of the United States" written by Frederick Douglass. It stated, in part:

We want the elective franchise in all the States now in the Union, and the same in all such States as may come into the Union hereafter. We believe that the highest welfare of this great country will be found in erasing from its statute-books all enactments discriminating in favor of or against any class of its people, and by establishing one law for the white and colored people alike . . .

Formerly our petitions for the elective franchise were met and denied upon the ground, that, while colored men were protected in person and property, they were not required to perform military duty . . . But now even this frivolous . . . apology for excluding us from the ballot-box is entirely swept away. Two hundred thousand colored men, according to a recent statement of President Lincoln, are now in the service, upon field and flood, in the army and the navy of the United States; and every day adds to their number . . .

In a republican country, where general suffrage is the rule, personal liberty, the right to testify in courts of law, the right to hold, buy, and sell property, become mere privileges, held at the option of others, where we are excepted from the general political liberty . . .

The possession of that right [the ballot] is the keystone to the arch of human liberty . . . We are men, and want to be as free in our native country as other men.

The convention organized a National Equal Rights League, and soon there were state branches in several Northern and Southern states. The leagues lost no time in presenting their demands to the people. The *Colored Citizen*, a black newspaper in Cincinnati and official mouthpiece for the Ohio Equal Rights League, stated:

For once let the colored men of the nation speak with one voice. Let California and Maine, Ohio and Louisiana join hands in demanding that in the new order of things which shall arise after this war, when the nation shall again clothe itself in the garments of peace, that there shall be no distinction on account of color in all our broad land.

After a meeting of the Louisiana Equal Rights League in January 1865, a new black paper, *La Tribune de la Nouvelle Orleans* (*The New Orleans Tribune*), proclaimed:

Emancipation is one fact, and effective liberty is another. Man does not have all his rights and privileges, he does not have free exercise of his faculties and skills by the simple consequence of the abolition of slavery. Old attitudes survive the proclamation of liberty, and old interests persist through the changes brought about by a new regime. After slavery has disappeared from the law, the former rulers seem to want to preserve slavery in fact . . . This party accepts emancipation, it is true; but it wants the black to be happy with an empty liberty. Such liberty would be but a word; we want true liberty . . .

Does America want to hold the black suspended between slavery and freedom, in a sphere where he possesses neither the right to live according to his wishes, nor the power to act by himself? No Pariahs [lower castes] in America! Such is the cry that should arise from every throat. Liberty is one and there is only one way to exercise it. Liberty must be the same for all men. If liberty is qualified, those who possess the least rights are not really free. We demand, therefore, like all the other citizens, and on the same footing as they:

The right to come and to go;

The right to vote;

The right to public instruction;

The right to hold public office;

The right to be judged, treated and governed according to the common law;

This is our program. May all who are worthy of exercising these rights join us in fighting for them.

As the war neared its end, the *Christian Recorder* urged African-Americans to redouble their efforts for equality:

Colored Men! Fellow Citizens of America! AWAKE TO ACTION!! . . . *As tax-payers, and loyal subjects of a Free Republican Government, let us contend lawfully, rightfully and perseveringly for our political rights . . . We have feasted on celebrations enough to go on and do a little more work* . . . No shouting yet! Go on and complete the victory!

These appeals and others were eventually answered with the Reconstruction Acts of 1867 and the Fifteenth Amendment in 1870 which finally granted suffrage to African-Americans.

This was a great achievement, culminating the expansion of suffrage (for men) that had begun in the 1820s and anticipating the enfranchisement of women by the Nineteenth Amendment half a century later in 1920. But after exercising the vote in large numbers during Reconstruction in the 1870s, most blacks lost the right to vote in the South by illegal and discriminatory state actions for nearly a century, until new federal legislation in the 1960s finally enforced the promise of the Fifteenth Amendment.

12

FORTY ACRES
AND A
SCHOOLHOUSE

At the beginning of the Civil War, more than 90% of the slaves could not read or write. The law forbade teaching slaves. A few had learned secretly, in defiance of law, but the great mass was illiterate. Nor, in the South, were there public schools for free blacks, so many of them were also illiterate. When freedom came, the first thing most Southern blacks wanted was education, for themselves and especially for their children.

Thousands of Southern black soldiers in the Union army were already using their spare time in camp to learn to read and write. As one example, Frances Beecher, wife of the commanding officer of the Thirty-fifth U.S. Colored Infantry, spent her mornings

teaching the men of our regiment to read and write, and it became my pleasing duty and habit, wherever our moving tents were pitched, there to set up our school. Sometimes the chaplain assisted, and sometimes the officers; and the result was that when the men came to be mustered out each one of them could proudly sign his name to the pay-roll in a good legible hand. When enlisted, all but two or three of

Black soldiers seated with white officers
and schoolteachers standing behind them
(Library of Congress)

*them were obliged to put a mark to their names as written
by the paymaster, thus:*

his
John X Jones
mark

*while their eagerness to learn and the difficulty that many
found in learning were very touching. One bright mulatto
man particularly worked at his letters for two years, and
then could only write his own name; while others learned
at once. Whenever they had a spare moment, out would
come a spelling-book or a primer or Testament, and you
would often see a group of heads around one book.*

In her memoirs Susie King, the young slave who had
escaped to a Union blockade ship off the Georgia coast in
1862, also gave a description of what it was like teaching
the freed slaves, both children and soldiers:

*After I had been on St. Simon's [Island] about three days,
Commodore Goldsborough heard of me, and came to Gas-
ton Bluff to see me. I found him very cordial. He said
Capain Whitmore had spoken to him of me, and that he
was pleased to hear of my being so capable, etc., and wished
me to take charge of a school for the children on the island.
I told him I would gladly do so, if I could have some more
books. He said I should have them, and in a week or two I
received two large boxes of books and Testaments from the
North. I had about forty children to teach, beside a number
of adults who came to me nights, all of them so eager to
learn to read, to read above anything else.*

Later transferred to Port Royal Island, King served as
a laundress and teacher for the First South Carolina
Volunteers. She recalled:

*I taught a great many of the comrades in Company E to
read and write, when they were off duty. Nearly all were
anxious to learn. My husband [she married a black soldier
named Taylor] taught some also when it was convenient*

for him. I was very happy to know my efforts were success-
ful in camp, and also felt grateful for the appreciation of
my services. I gave my services willingly for four years and
three months without receiving a dollar. I was glad, how-
ever, to be allowed to go with the regiment, to care for the
sick and afflicted comrades.

Contrabands, soldiers, ex-slaves and children—they
hungered and thirsted for education. As early as 1863,
Rev. Thomas Calahan, a Northern Presbyterian missionary serving among freed slaves in Louisiana, wrote:

You have no idea of the state of things here. Go out in
any direction and you meet negroes on horses, negroes on
mules, negroes with oxen, negroes by the wagon, cart and
buggy load, negroes on foot, men, women, and children;
negroes in uniform, negroes in rags, negroes in frame
houses, negroes living in tents, negroes living in rail pens
covered with brush, and negroes living on the bare ground
with the sky for their covering; all hopeful, almost all
cheerful, every one pleading to be taught, willing to do
anything for learning. They are never out of our rooms, and
their cry is for "Books! Books!" and "when will school
begin?" Negro women come and offer to cook and wash for
us, if we will only teach them to read the Bible . . . And
think of people living in brush tents gathering for the
prayer meetings that last far into the night. Every night
hymns of praise to God and prayers for the Government
that oppressed them so long, rise around us on every side
prayers for the white teachers that have already come—
prayers that God would send them more.

Many white men and women, most of them former
abolitionists, gave up comfortable homes in the North to
come South and teach the freedpeople to read and write.
Nearly every Northern city organized a "freedmen's aid
society," and most Northern churches helped support
Christian missionaries and teachers. One of the earliest
freedmen's aid enterprises was carried out on the South
Carolina Sea Islands, which were captured by Union
forces in November 1861. By early 1862, the first teachers

had reached the islands and opened schools for the contra-bands. Children attending during the day, and many adults came in the evening after working in the fields all day.

Most of the teachers from the North were white, but several Northern blacks also came. One among those on the Sea Islands was Charlotte Forten, a woman from a distinguished Philadelphia black family. Forten had been teaching in the Massachusetts public schools for several years before she decided to go South and teach freedpeople in 1862. She later wrote about her experiences:

The first day at school was rather trying. Most of my children were very small, and consequently restless. Some were too young to learn the alphabet. These little ones were brought to school because the older children—in whose care their parents leave them while at work—could not come without them. We were therefore willing to have them come, although they seemed to have discovered the secret of perpetual motion, and tried one's patience sadly. But after some days of positive, though not severe treatment, order was brought out of chaos, and I found but little difficulty in managing and quieting the tiniest and most restless spirits. I never before saw children so eager to learn, although I had had several years' experience in New England schools. Coming to school is a constant delight and recreation to them. They come here as other children go to play. The older ones, during the summer, work in the fields from early morning until eleven or twelve o'clock, and then come into school, after their hard toil in the hot sun, as bright and as anxious to learn as ever.

Of course there are some stupid ones, but these are in the minority. The majority learn with wonderful rapidity. Many of the grown people are desirous of learning to read. It is wonderful how a people who have been so long crushed to the earth, so imbruted as these have been—and they are said to be among the most degraded negroes of the South— can have so great a desire for knowledge, and such a capability for attaining it . . .

The tiniest children are delighted to get a book in their hands. Many of them already know their letters. The par-

*ents are eager to have them learn. They sometimes said to
me,—"Do, Miss, let de chil'en learn eberyting dey can. We
nebber hab no chance to learn nuttin', but we wants de
chil'en to learn."*

*They are willing to make many sacrifices that their
children may attend school. One old woman, who had a
large family of children, came regularly to school in the
winter, and took her seat among the little ones. She was at
least sixty years old. Another woman—who had one of the
best faces I ever saw—came daily, and brought her baby in
her arms . . .*

Others who came to the Sea Islands included the first
black missionaries to the South—Reverend James Lynch
of Baltimore and Reverend James D. Hall of New York,
sent by the African Methodist Episcopal Church in May
1863. The Church also sent several black women teachers
South during the war.

When schoolhouses began to be established, African-
Americans were among the pioneers in founding them.
A freedwoman, Mary Chase of Alexandria, Virginia,
started the first contraband school in the South on
September 1, 1861. Soon, Alexandria blacks had opened
more schools for freedpeople. At about the same time, on
September 17, 1861, Mrs. Mary Peake, a free Negro of
Hampton, Virginia, started a school for ex-slaves at
Fortress Monroe. The African Civilization Society of
New York, founded in 1858 to promote African-Ameri-
can missionary effort and settlement in Africa, reorgan-
ized during the Civil War as a freedmen's aid association
and between 1864 and 1867 established six black schools
in Washington, D.C.

These are but a few examples of the contributions to
education made during the war. After the war, of course,
the scope of freedmen's education was much enlarged, and
many more schools, academies and colleges were established in the South. But all these institutions had their
origin in the desire for education awakened in the minds
of ex-slaves during the Civil War. In that four-year period,
it was estimated that more than 200,000 freedpeople had
begun attending school.

Beyond the strict ABCs, the masses of liberated Southern blacks also needed education in more practical matters, as well as some kind of financial help. Here, the freedmen's aid societies played a significant role. The societies conducted classes in home economics for women and taught freedmen better methods of farming. And sometimes they provided food and clothing for hungry blacks who owned nothing but the rags they wore.

Although most of these freedmen's aid societies were organized and financed by Northern whites (because most Northern blacks were poor), black people in the North did not shirk financial responsibility for their emancipated brothers and sisters. In every Northern city was a sizable African-American population, the black churches and societies formed freedmen's aid associations. One, the Contraband Relief Association of Washington, was organized by Elizabeth Keckley, Mrs. Lincoln's seamstress.

Born a slave in Virginia, Mrs. Keckley had in the 1840s moved to St. Louis, where she worked as a dressmaker to purchase freedom for herself and her son. Later, living in Washington, she came to the attention of Mrs. Lincoln, and in 1861 became the First Lady's seamstress. Intelligent, sensitive and sympathetic, Mrs. Keckley soon became a close friend of the president's wife. Her son joined the Union army and was killed on a battlefield in Missouri. In a book about her experiences in the White House during the war, Mrs. Keckley described the founding of the Contraband Relief Association of Washington in 1862:

One fair summer evening I was walking the streets of Washington, accompanied by a friend, when a band of music was heard in the distance. We wondered what it could mean, and curiosity prompted us to find out ... We approached the sentinel on duty at the gate [of Mrs. Farnham's house], and asked what was going on. He told us that it was a festival given for the benefit of the sick and wounded soldiers in the city. This suggested an idea to me. If the white people can give festivals to raise funds for the relief of suffering soldiers, why should not the well-to-do colored people go to work to do something for the benefit of the suffering blacks? I could not rest. The thought was ever present with me, and the next Sunday I made a suggestion in the colored church, that a society of colored people be formed to labor for the benefit of the unfortunate freedmen. The idea proved popular, and in two weeks "the Contraband Relief Association" was organized, with forty working members . . .

I told Mrs. Lincoln of my project; and she immediately headed my list with a subscription of $200. I circulated among the colored people, and got them thoroughly interested in the subject, when I was called to Boston by Mrs. Lincoln, who wished to visit her son Robert, attending college in that city. I met Mr. Wendell Phillips, and other Boston philanthropists, who gave me all the assistance in their power. We held a mass meeting at the Colored Baptist Church, Rev. Mr. Grimes, in Boston, raised a sum of money, and organized there a branch society . . .

Returning to New York, we held a successful meeting at the Shiloh Church, Rev. Henry Highland Garnet, pastor. The Metropolitan Hotel, at that time as now, employed colored help. I suggested the object of my mission to Robert Thompson, Steward of the Hotel, who immediately raised quite a sum of money among the dining-room waiters. Mr. Frederick Douglass contributed $200, besides lecturing for us. Other prominent colored men sent in liberal contributions. From England, a large quantity of stores was received. Mrs. Lincoln made frequent contributions, as also did the President.

Thus, in the face of a whole social revolution, private citizens, both black and white, responded—with freedmen's aid associations, as teachers and in whatever ways they could. But many blacks argued that these things were not yet enough to start freedmen on the new life. Without some kind of large-scale economic assistance also, they said, the ex-slave would remain a sharecropper or laborer on the land of his former master.

Since most of the freedpeople had lived on plantations all their lives and would remain farmers, the best way to promote their economic independence was to help them become landowners—to help them get "forty acres and a mule." Some blacks urged the government to seize rebel

*Black and white teachers of a freedpeople's school in
the South during the Civil War* (U.S. Army Military
History Institute)

plantations under the confiscation laws and divide them up among freed slaves. Others wanted the government to lend freedmen the money to buy land. Prince Rivers, a black sergeant in the First South Carolina Volunteers, said in November 1863 that "every colored man will be a slave, and feel himself a slave until he can raise him own bale of cotton and put him own mark on it and say dis is mine!" And Daniel Foster, an abolitionist colonel of the Third North Carolina Colored Volunteers, wrote in January 1864:

The slaves, with almost entire unanimity, long for a little land, that they may own a home of their own. I trust the Government will make provision for them to buy land when they wish. Let these immense plantations in the South be cut up, and the soil sold at a low rate, to industrious freedmen.

The Union government did little to help blacks acquire land of their own, but freedmen often managed to get hold of a few acres one way or another during the war. Whenever the Union army moved into a new district, most of the Southern whites fled, abandoning their farms and plantations. Contrabands were often put to work on these plantations to raise cotton or other crops under the guidance of Northern labor superintendents, who paid them wages. The Union government seized thousands of acres of Southern land for nonpayment of taxes, and some of it, especially on the South Carolina Sea Islands, was put up for auction. Blacks and their friends wanted the government to give freedmen the first chance to buy the property, at special low prices, but the Lincoln administration refused. Instead, the land was sold at open auction and was bought up chiefly by wealthy speculators and investors from the North.

Blacks who had saved some money but were unable to pay competitive prices for the land they had worked on most of their lives were sadly disappointed. An old freedman on the South Carolina Sea Islands dictated a letter to a former teacher who had returned to Philadelphia. His words, put down exactly as dictated, retain the Sea Island dialect.

MY DEAR YOUNG MISSUS: *I been a elder in de church, and speretual fader to a hep of gals no older dan oona [you]. I know dat womens has feelin' hearts, and dat de men will heardy de voice of a gal when dey too hard head for mind dose dat has more wisdom. So I bin a beg one of dese yere little white sisters in the church, dat the Lord sends from the Nort for school we chilen, to write oona for me to ax of oona if oona so please an' will be so kind, my missus, to speak to Linkum and tell him for we how we po' folks tank him and de Lord for we great privilege to see de happy day when we can talk to de white folks and make known to de Gov'ment what we wants. Do, my missus, tell Linkum dat we wants land—dis bery land dat is rich wid de sweat ob we face and de blood ob we back. We born here; we parents' graves here; we donne oder country; dis yere our home. De Nort folks hab home, antee? What a pity dat dey don't love der home like we love we home, for den dey would neber come here for buy all way from we.*

Do, my missus, beg Linkum for lef us room for buy land and live here. We don't ask for it for notins. We too tankful. We too satisfy to pay just what de rich buckra [white man] pay. But dey done buy too much a'ready, and lef we no chance. We could a bin buy all we want, but dey make de lots too big, and cut we out . . .

Do missus speak ter um for we, an' ax Linkum for stretch out he hand and make dese yer missionaries [tax commissioners] cut de land so dat we able for buy. Dey good and wise men, may be, but ax Linkum for send us his word, and den we satisfy. Our men—ebery able bodied man from we island—bin a fight for dere country in Florida, at Fort Wagner; any where dat Govment send um. But dis dere country. Dey want land here, for dere wives to work. Look at de fiels! No more but womens and chilens, all de men gone to fight, and while dey gone de land sold from dere families to rich white buckra to scrape, and neber live on. Dey runs to de North; dey can't live here. What dey want to carry from we all de witeness of de land, and leave we for Govment to feed . . .

Speak softly next time you meets Massa Linkum. Talk him bout me, and de Lord will keep you warm under he feathers, he will gather oona to he breast, for he love dem what help de poor.

Lincoln was unable to satisfy their requests, but in later years Sea Island blacks did manage to buy several thousand acres from the original Northern wartime purchasers. Meanwhile, there occurred one example of a truly revolutionary land reform.

As General Sherman marched through Georgia in the last weeks of 1864, thousands of ragged contrabands fell in behind his troops. When the army reached Savannah, the problem of taking care of the refugees became critical. Sherman and Secretary of War Stanton held a conference with 20 black ministers and church officials of Savannah, 15 of them former slaves. In response to one of Stanton's questions, the spokesman for the blacks replied, "The way we can best take care of ourselves is to have land, and turn it and till it by our labor . . . We want to be placed on land until we are able to buy it, and make it our own."

Four days later, Sherman issued his "Special Field Order Number 15," which designated the coastline and riverbanks 30 miles inland from Charleston to Jacksonville as an area for black settlement. Freedmen settling in this area could take not more than 40 acres of land per family, to which they would be given temporary title until Congress granted them permanent legal title. By the end of June 1865, more than 40,000 freedpeople had moved onto their new farms.

But this great experiment was destroyed by Lincoln's successor, President Andrew Johnson, who in August 1865 pardoned the former Confederate owners and restored the property to them. The majority of the 40,000 blacks were turned off their farms, some at bayonet point, and forced to work for white plantation owners. It was a tragic ending.

Thus, while the government had freed the slaves, it did little to help them get on their feet. Without the opportunity to make a decent living, the blacks' freedom was only partial, and the unhappy consequences of that partial freedom are still with us today.

13

"WAS THE WAR IN VAIN?"

The "Negro Question" was one of the main issues of the Civil War. The South went to war in 1861 to protect itself against what it considered a Northern threat to "Southern Institutions." In a speech at Savannah, Georgia on March 21 of that year, Alexander Stephens, Vice-President of the Confederacy, declared: "Our Confederacy is founded upon . . . the great truth that the black is not equal to the white man. That slavery—subordination to the superior race, is his natural and normal condition. This, our new Government, is the first, in the history of the world, based upon this great physical and moral truth."

Although the South fought to preserve slavery, the North did not at first fight to destroy the "peculiar institution." Its aim was to restore the Union. Nevertheless, from the fall of Fort Sumter to the surrender at Appomattox, the question of the African-American's status in a restored Union was an issue of much concern. By 1862, it had become apparent that the war would bring great changes for black people, and their hopes grew. A black from California expressed it this way:

Everything around us indicates a change in our condition, and the revolution of events, and the change in the public sentiment toward us, all go to prove the necessity for us to prepare to act in a different sphere from that in which we have heretofore acted . . . The only place the American historian could find for the colored man was in the background of a cotton-field, or the foreground of a canebrake or a rice swamp, to adorn the pages of geography . . . But . . . old things are passing away, and eventually old prejudices must follow. The revolution has begun, and time alone must decide where it is to end.

Abolitionists argued that the North could not win the war, or establish a just peace, unless it abolished slavery, and by 1863 President Lincoln had come to agree. With his Emancipation Proclamation, the war entered a new phase; the abolition of slavery became a war aim closely linked to the restoration of the Union.

Robert Purvis voiced black people's exultation at the change of events in a speech to the American Anti-Slavery Society in May of that year. Purvis, despite his wealth and fine home in a Philadelphia suburb, was a militant and radical black leader. In the past, he had frequently denounced the United States because it supported slavery, but now he said:

This is a proud day for the "colored" man. For the first time since this Society was organized, I stand before you a recognized citizen of the United States . . . You know, Mr. Chairman, how bitterly I used to denounce the United States as the basest despotism the sun ever shone upon; and I take nothing back that ever I said. When this government was, as it used to be, a slaveholding oligarchy . . . I hated it with a wrath which words could not express, and I denounced it with all the bitterness of my indignant soul . . . I was a victim, stricken, degraded, injured, insulted in my person, in my family, in my friends, in my estate; I returned bitterness for bitterness, and scorn for scorn . . . [But now] I forget the past; joy fills my soul at the prospect of the future . . .

The good time which has so long been coming is at hand. I feel it, I see it in the air, I read it in the signs of the times; I see it in the acts of Congress, in the abolition of slavery in

the District of Columbia, in its exclusion from the Territo-
ries . . . in the new spirit that is in the army; I see it in the
black regiment of South Carolina—(applause); I see it in
the 54th Regiment of Massachusetts; I see it in the order of
Adjutant-General Thomas, forming a black brigade at
Memphis; I see it, above all, and more than all, in THE
GLORIOUS AND IMMORTAL PROCLAMATION OF ABRAHAM LINCOLN
ON THE FIRST OF JANUARY, *1863 (cheers) . . . In spirit and in*
purpose, thanks to Almighty God! this is no longer a
slaveholding republic. The fiat has gone forth which, when
this rebellion is crushed . . . in the simple but beautiful
language of the President, "will take all burdens from off
all backs, and make every man a freeman."

The drive for emancipation was climaxed in 1865 by the
Thirteenth Amendment, which abolished slavery
throughout the nation. The Civil War had worked a revolution in the Negro's status; it brought freedom to
4,000,000 slaves, and set in motion forces that, in theory
at least, would bring equal civil and political rights to all
African-Americans. The war meant the beginnings of education for thousands of freedpeople in the South, and the
desegregation of schools and public facilities in many parts
of the North. An editorial in the *Christian Recorder*
summed it up:

When we reflect upon the condition and position of the
African race, at the present time, contrasted with that
presented to the inquisitive gaze of a world four years ago,
well may we boast of being in the ascendant . . . Within two
years the standard of "Justice" has been raised in our favor;
an admission of our valor, our manhood, our courage, has
been made by our former oppressors; partial equality has
been extended to us, and our rights as citizens have been
recognized . . . we are on the advance.

Little wonder that in 1865 blacks felt hopeful. But the
next four decades would see their hopes turned sour, their
expectations embittered. After federal troops withdrew
from the South and Reconstruction ended in the 1870s,
the white people of the South proceeded to segregate,

disfranchise, exploit and frequently lynch black people. Northern whites, who had fought side by side with black men to save the Union, grew indifferent to the plight of Southern blacks, while increasing *de facto* segregation made a mockery of equal rights laws in the North.

In 1902 Susie King Taylor, the former teacher of the First South Carolina Volunteers, wrote an analysis of the race issue in America that can perhaps stand as the best conclusion to a book on the blacks in the Civil War:

I wonder if our white fellow men realize the true sense or meaning of brotherhood? For two hundred years we had toiled for them; the war of 1861 came and was ended, and we thought our race was forever freed from bondage, and that the two races could live in unity with each other, but when we read almost every day of what is being done to my race by some whites in the South, I sometimes ask, "Was the war in vain? Has it brought freedom, in the full sense of the word, or has it not made our condition more hopeless?"

In this "land of the free" we are burned, tortured, and denied a fair trial, murdered for any imaginary wrong conceived in the brain of the negro-hating white man. There is no redress for us from a government which promised to protect all under its flag. It seems a mystery to me. They say, "One flag, one nation, one country indivisible." Is this true? Can we say this truthfully, when one race is allowed to burn, hang, and inflict the most horrible torture weekly, monthly, on another? No, we cannot sing, "My country, 'tis of thee, Sweet land of Liberty!" It is hollow mockery. The Southland laws are all on the side of the white, and they do just as they like to the negro . . .

I may not live to see it, but the time is approaching when the South will again have cause to repent for the blood it has shed of innocent black men, for their blood cries out for vengeance . . . All we ask for is "equal justice," the same that is accorded to all other races who come to this country.

BIBLIOGRAPHY

Three excellent general histories of African-Americans that include chapters on the Civil War are John Hope Franklin, *From Slavery to Freedom* (New York, Knopf, 1980); *Benjamin Quarles, *The Negro in the Making of America* (New York, Collier-Macmillan, 1969); and *August Meier and Elliott Rudwick, *From Plantation to Ghetto* (New York, Hill and Wang, 1976). *Herbert Aptheker, ed., *Documentary History of the Negro People in the United States* (2 vols., The Citadel Press, 1962), Volume I, pp. 459–532, contains many documents relating to the Negro's role in the conflict.

The most readable survey of all phases of the blacks in the Civil War is *Benjamin Quarles, *The Negro in the Civil War* (Boston, Little, Brown, 1953). There is some additional material in the same author's *Lincoln and the Negro* (New York, Oxford University Press, 1962). Another perspective is provided by Supreme Court Justice William O. Douglas, who has written *Mr. Lincoln and the Negroes: The Long Road to Equality* (New York, 1965). *James M. McPherson, *The Negro's Civil War* (Urbana, Ill, University of Illinois Press, 1982), tells the story of the black man in the conflict largely in the words of Negroes themselves. The same author's *The Struggle for Equality: Abolitionists and the Negro in the Civil War and Reconstruction*

Titles marked with * are available in paperback.

(Princeton, Princeton University Press, 1964) deals with the role of white and black abolitionists. *Bell I. Wiley, *Southern Negroes, 1861–1865* (New Haven, Yale University Press, 1965), is a thorough study of what happened to the slaves and free blacks of the South during the war. A rich study of black perceptions of the coming of freedom during and after the war is *Leon Litwack, *Been in the Storm So Long: The Aftermath of Slavery* (New York, Knopf, 1979). A wealth of documents, accompanied by explanatory and interpretive material, can be found in Ira Berlin, Barbara J. Fields, Thavolia Glymph, Joseph P. Reidy and Leslie L. Rowland, eds., *The Destruction of Slavery*, Series I, Volume I of *Freedom: A Documentary History of Emancipation* (Cambridge, Cambridge University Press, 1985). Two good studies of the wartime experiences of black people, slave and free, in two slave states are *Barbara Jeanne Fields, *Slavery and Freedom on the Middle Ground: Maryland during the Nineteenth Century* (New Haven, Yale University Press, 1985) and *Clarence L. Mohr, *On the Threshold of Freedom: Masters and Slaves in Civil War Georgia* (Athens, Ga., University of Georgia Press, 1986). The Union army's policy toward freed slaves is described in Louis S. Gerteis, *From Contraband to Freedman* (Westport, Conn., Greenwood Press, 1973).

The best introduction to the story of black soldiers is *Dudley T. Cornis, *The Sable Arm: Negro Troops in the Union Army, 1861–1865* (New York, Norton, 1966). *Thomas Wentworth Higginson, *Army Life in a Black Regiment* (New York, 1962), is a fascinating story of one regiment of former slaves by their white commander. A readable account of the Massachusetts Fifty-fourth Regiment is Peter Burchard, *One Gallant Rush: Robert Gould Shaw and his Brave Black Regiment* (New York, St. Martin's Press, 1965). The movie *Glory*, released in 1989, is a dramatization of the story of the Fifty-fourth Massachusetts. For a great number of documents and accompanying explanatory material about black soldiers during the war, see Ira Berlin and Joseph P. Reidy and Leslie Rowland, eds., *The Black Military Experience*, Series II of *Freedom: A Documentary History of Emancipation* (Cambridge, Cambridge University Press, 1982). An excellent study of the relationship between black soldiers and their white officers is Joseph T. Glatthaar, *Forged in Battle: The Civil War Alliance of Black Soldiers and White Officers* (New York, Free Press, 1990). For the debate in the South on arming slaves to fight for the Confederacy, see Robert F. Durden, ed., *The Gray and the Black: The Confederate Debate on Emancipation* (Baton Rouge, Louisiana State University Press, 1972).

For those who are interested in the education of freedpeople, the diary of a Northern black woman who went to the South Carolina Sea Islands to teach former slaves makes interesting reading: *Ray Allen Billington, ed., *The Journal of Charlotte Forten* (New York, Collier Books, 1961). The autobiography of the most famous ex-slave includes considerable material on the Civil War: *Frederick Douglass, *Life and Times of Frederick Douglass* (New York, Collier Books, 1962). Volume III of Philip S. Foner, *The Life and Writings of Frederick Douglass* (4 vols., New York, International Publishers, 1950–1955), reprints most of Douglass' important speeches, editorials and letters from the Civil War years. An excellent modern biography of Douglass is *Benjamin Quarles, *Frederick Douglass* (New York, Atheneum, 1968).

In the 1930s a team of interviewers talked with many old Negroes in the South about their memories of slavery, and some of these aged ex-slaves gave lively and entertaining accounts of their experiences as young slaves during the Civil War. These talks are printed in Parts IV and V of *Benjamin A. Botkin, ed., *Lay My Burden Down: A Folk History of Slavery* (Chicago, University of Chicago Press, 1965). The Civil War produced a good number of songs by and about African-Americans; some of these can be found in Irwin Silber, ed., *Songs of the Civil War* (New York, Columbia University Press, 1960).

Some of the most interesting and significant passages in this book are taken from newspapers edited by blacks during the Civil War. The most important of these newspapers were: *The Anglo-African*, published in New York; the *Christian Recorder*, the newspaper of the African Methodist Episcopal Church, issued in Philadelphia; *Douglass' Monthly*, edited and published by Frederick

Douglass in Rochester, New York; *L'Union* (*The Union*), issued by New Orleans Negroes from 1862 to 1864; and *La Tribune de la Nouvelle Orleans* (*The New Orleans Tribune*), which succeeded *L'Union*. These two New Orleans newspapers were printed half in English and half in French, because many of the blacks in New Orleans, like many of the whites, were French-speaking descendants of the original settlers of Louisiana.

A large number of pamphlets, autobiographies and contemporary books by and about blacks in the Civil War were consulted with profit. Several manuscript collections of personal and official letters by both blacks and whites produced some valuable items. The federal government has published a huge number of official reports and volumes on all aspects of the Civil War, and some of these were consulted for material about the freedpeople and about black soldiers. The Slave Narratives, collected by the Federal Writers' Project in the 1930s and deposited in the Rare Book Division of the Library of Congress, also provided several items of interest. These narratives have been published in George P. Rawick, ed., *The American Slave: A Composite Autobiography*, 19 vols. (Westport, Conn., Greenwood Press, 1972), and in a 12-volume supplement (1977).

INDEX

JAMES M. McPHERSON lives in Princeton, New Jersey, where he is Edwards Professor of American History at Princeton University. He has written a half-dozen books on the history of race relations in the 19th century and on the Civil War era of American history, including *Battle Cry of Freedom: The Civil War Era*, which won the Pulitzer Prize in history for 1989.